# The ISO 9000 Workbook

# The ISO 9000 Workbook

## A Comprehensive Guide to Developing Quality Manuals and Procedures

# Greg Hutchins

omneo

AN IMPRINT OF OLIVER WIGHT PUBLICATIONS, INC.
*85 Allen Martin Drive*
*Essex Junction, VT 05452*

Copyright © 1994 by Greg Hutchins

Published by Oliver Wight Publications, Inc.

All rights reserved. This book or any parts thereof may not
be reproduced without permission from the publisher.

Oliver Wight Publications books may be purchased for educational, business, or
sales promotional use. For information, please call or write: Special Sales Department,
Oliver Wight Publications, Inc., 85 Allen Martin Drive, Essex Junction, VT 05452.
Telephone: (800) 343-0625 or (802) 878-8161; FAX: (802) 878-3384.

ISBN 0-939246-73-2
ISBN 0-471142-45-X(pbk)

1  2  3  4  5  6  7  8  9  10

# CONTENTS

| | |
|---|---|
| **PREFACE** | ix |
| **HOW TO WRITE QUALITY DOCUMENTATION** | **1** |
| The Quality Manual and Its Policies | 3 |
| Numbering the Quality Manual | 6 |
| How to Develop Quality Policies and Procedures | 10 |
| Managing Quality Documentation | 18 |
| Tips for Developing the Quality Manual | 20 |
| Lack of Quality Documentation | 23 |
| Quality Documentation | 25 |
| **SAMPLE QUALITY MANUALS** | **29** |
| QUALITY MANUAL 1 | 31 |
| QUALITY MANUAL 2 | 47 |
| QUALITY MANUAL 3 | 69 |
| QUALITY MANUAL 4 | 91 |
| **SAMPLE QUALITY PROCEDURES** | **97** |
| ISO 9001 Clause 4.1: Management Responsibility | 99 |
| *Quality Department Organization* | 99 |
| ISO 9001 Clause 4.2: Quality System | 101 |
| *Quality Planning* | 101 |
| *Quality Systems Planning* | 102 |
| ISO 9001 Clause 4.3: Contract Review | 104 |
| *New Contract Requirements* | 104 |

| | |
|---|---|
| ISO 9001 Clause 4.4: Design Control | 106 |
| *Engineering Drawing Review* | 106 |
| *Design Review, Documentation Review, and Control* | 107 |
| *Design Review Process* | 108 |
| ISO 9001 Clause 4.5: Document and Data Control | 110 |
| *Quality Records and Documentation Control* | 110 |
| ISO 9001 Clause 4.6: Purchasing | 111 |
| *Purchasing Controls* | 111 |
| *Supplier Quality Evaluation* | 112 |
| ISO 9001 Clause 4.7: Control of Customer-Supplied Product | 114 |
| *Use of Customer Property* | 114 |
| *Control of Customer Property* | 115 |
| ISO 9001 Clause 4.8: Product Identification and Traceability | 116 |
| *Product Traceability* | 116 |
| ISO 9001 Clause 4.9: Process Control | 117 |
| *Process Control* | 117 |
| *First-Article Inspection* | 118 |
| ISO 9001 Clause 4.10: Inspection and Testing | 119 |
| *Receiving Inspection* | 119 |
| *In-Process Inspection* | 122 |
| *Final Inspection* | 123 |
| *Final Testing* | 124 |
| ISO 9001 Clause 4.11: Control of Inspection, Measuring, and Test Equipment | 125 |
| *Calibration System Control* | 125 |
| ISO 9001 4.12: Inspection and Test Status | 127 |
| ISO 9001 4.13: Control of Nonconforming Product | 128 |
| *Handling Nonconforming Materials* | 128 |
| ISO 9001 4.14: Corrective and Preventive Action | 130 |
| *Corrective Action Requests* | 130 |
| ISO 9001 Clause 4.15: Handling, Storage, Packaging, Preservation, and Delivery | 131 |
| *Packaging, Handling, and Shipping Responsibilities* | 131 |
| *Handling, Storage, Preservation, and Shipment* | 132 |

| | |
|---|---|
| ISO 9001 Clause 4.16: Control of Quality Records | 133 |
|    *Quality Records* | 133 |
| ISO 9001 Clause 4.17: Internal Quality Audits | 134 |
|    *Internal Quality Audits* | 134 |
|    *Customer Audit and Inspection* | 135 |
| ISO 9001 Clause 4.18: Training | 137 |
|    *Quality Training Procedure* | 137 |
| ISO 9001 Clause 4.19: Servicing | 138 |
|    *After-Sales Servicing* | 138 |
| ISO 9001 Clause 4.20: Statistical Techniques | 139 |
|    *Process Capability Study* | 139 |

# SAMPLE QUALITY FORMS      141

| | |
|---|---|
| Acknowledgment of Quality Policies and Procedures | 143 |
| Approved Supplier List | 144 |
| Calibration Record | 145 |
| Corrective Action Request (CAR) | 146 |
| Corrective Action Status Report | 147 |
| Customer-Supplied Equipment | 148 |
| Employee Quality Training | 149 |
| First-Piece Inspection | 150 |
| Handling, Storage, Packaging, and Delivery Requirements and Instructions | 151 |
| Inspection Instructions | 152 |
| ISO 9000 Quality Policies | 153 |
| ISO 9001 Preassessment Checklist | 154 |
| ISO 9001 Quality Evaluation Checklist | 163 |
| Machined Parts Instruction Form | 164 |
| New Product Analysis | 165 |
| Nonconforming Materials and Parts Report | 166 |
| Nonconforming Materials Master Log | 167 |
| Organizational Commitment Statement | 168 |
| Process and Production Instructions | 169 |

| | |
|---|---:|
| Process, Production, Inspection, and Measurement Equipment Maintenance | 170 |
| Quality Assurance Plan | 171 |
| Quality Manual Approval List | 172 |
| Quality Manual Table of Contents | 173 |
| Quality Policies Approval and Review Chart | 174 |
| Receiving, In-Process, and Final Inspection Instructions | 176 |
| Waiver or Deviation Request | 177 |

**GLOSSARY**      **179**

**INDEX**      **185**

# PREFACE

This is a "do it yourself" workbook or, as my editor likes to call it, an implementation guide. Its purpose is to allow you to develop a quality manual and lower-level documents that satisfy the requirements of ISO 9001/9002/9003.

The goal of this book is to simplify the documentation development process by offering quality documentation that worked for companies that already have secured ISO 9000 registration. Anyone can do it and satisfy the registrar's auditor, your customers, and most important, yourself.

Quality documentation may initially be written to satisfy ISO 9000 requirements or, as some would say, to appease the registrar's auditors. But the primary purpose for developing the documentation is to make your operations more efficient and effective.

Quality documentation can help to make your operations, processes, and systems more consistent by ensuring that

- Customer requirements are understood and defined,

- Customer requirements are internalized into the company,

- Critical product attributes are identified,

- Critical process parameters related to these attributes are identified,

- Processes are in control, capable, and improving,

- Operational methods are consistent and documented,

- Operators are trained in these methods,

- Operations and systems are monitored and audited, and

- Symptoms and root causes of deviations are corrected.

## WHAT DOES THIS BOOK DO FOR YOU?

This book provides you with the following benefits. It

- Provides four comprehensive examples of quality manuals,
- Provides many examples of quality procedures and specific tips for developing your own documentation,
- Provides examples of quality forms,
- Clarifies the key terms and concepts used in the ISO 9000 universe, and
- Identifies approaches that have worked with ISO 9000–registered companies.

## ORGANIZATION OF THIS BOOK

This book is divided into the following major parts:

- How to write quality documentation,
- Sample quality manuals,
- Sample quality procedures, and
- Sample quality forms.

Many small companies already have human resource policies and procedures that address employment and personnel management issues, such as sexual harassment, as required by law. These companies are now finding that they need quality policies, procedures, and work instructions, often because a customer requires a quality program or ISO 9000 certification.

If you already have quality documents, don't develop ISO 9000 documentation from scratch. It is much easier if you have templates or examples of what the documents should look like. This book and its accompanying software are a toolbox for developing this documentation. This documentation toolbox can help you to

- Develop quality policies and procedures if none exist,
- Assist you in developing ISO 9000 specific procedures if you have other quality systems, and
- Establish quality systems where none exist.

The ISO 9000 policies, procedures, and forms are generic so that you can rewrite the quality documentation to fit your specific requirements. Once the quality manual is developed, you should have your registrar or a quality consultant review it to ensure that it complies with all ISO 9001/9002/9003 requirements. When preparing your quality manual, follow the format outlined in this book, and insert only those documents that apply to your operations.

The more detailed quality documentation—such as procedures, work instructions, and forms—will have to be tailored to your specific applications, processes, systems, and products.

# HOW TO WRITE QUALITY DOCUMENTATION

# THE QUALITY MANUAL AND ITS POLICIES

According to ISO 8402, Quality Management and Quality Assurance Vocabulary, a quality manual is a document that defines generic company policies and describes its quality systems. A quality manual is usually a generic document that can be used as marketing or informational documentation. A quality manual normally contains information that can be used by customers, third-party registrars, and other outside parties. In some cases, because a quality manual contains proprietary or sensitive information, it will have restricted distribution.

Quality policies inform employees, stakeholders, and suppliers about organizational goals to ensure overall consistency within the company.

*Procedures* set requirements or rules for ensuring and controlling quality. *Work, inspection,* or other types of *instructions* are sequential rules of required actions for ensuring and controlling quality. Work instructions usually distill the best operational practices for maintaining quality.

*Policies*, by their nature, are different than procedures and work instructions. Policies are guides for organizational behavior. There may be some latitude or discretion in interpreting or implementing a policy. Policies define activities or systems for making decisions. The desired consequence is to have products and services satisfy customers. The systems and processes that deliver these products and services should be stable, capable, and continuously improving.

Policies usually allow for individual discretion. Depending on the circumstances, policies are living documents that can be changed or rewritten to fit particular situations. Policies usually are general documents that are developed to fit most circumstances. When policies don't fit a special situation, then individual discretion, knowledge, and judgment should dictate action.

Quality policies should reinforce the organization's overall goals, objectives, and plans. They should provide enough flexibility within a framework of accepted activities to have uniform managerial, team, and individual decisions and outcomes. If situations are similar, then decisions should be similar. If situations are different, then the decision-making process should consider the same factors to arrive at predictable decisions with similar outcomes.

As the quality issue becomes more important, day-to-day challenges can be met by quality policies, procedures, and work instructions that serve as guides to employees, customers, and suppliers.

Quality policies that reflect organizational consensus minimize the chances that unusual situations will occur or recur. All employees should understand and be guided by the common principles and precepts of the quality policies. Policies serve as a consistent guide: if there are unusual occurrences, then a mechanism is available for obtaining support, advice, or resources; if there are quality system deficiencies, then an internal audit system is available for exploring the nature of the problem, and a corrective action quality system ensures they don't recur.

Quality system policies also are empowering tools. The organization commits itself and its suppliers to having quality systems, being accountable for them, and correcting them if there are deficiencies. Employees are accountable and also have the authority to act. With ISO 9000 quality systems, a management representative also is responsible for the quality system implementation.

Quality system policies ensure that quality systems are in place and working properly and that everyone is responsible for quality. If the policies represent an organizational consensus, then all employees should be treated fairly and similarly because all will follow the same policies and procedures.

## BENEFITS OF A QUALITY MANUAL

ISO 9000 quality policies are compiled into a companywide quality manual. The quality manual has important uses:

- *Training manual.* The manual can be used to introduce new employees to the organization, its culture, its structure, and its beliefs. The procedures manual and work instructions can be used to train supervisors, teams, and individuals in what and how work should be done.

- *Communications vehicle.* Quality policies can be used as a marketing tool for communicating with customers about quality commitment. If quality policies are formulated through organizational review and consensus, then all the organization's stakeholders can understand the organization's position on quality issues.

- *Culture device.* The process of developing quality policies can be used to communicate with employees about company values, ethics, and beliefs. The policies can establish consensus on company quality commitment and beliefs. If quality policies are drafted, approved, and circulated through consensus, then all employees understand the organization's position or recommended practices.

The quality manual also can be used for a number of other purposes:

- Indicating compliance with ISO 9000 quality requirements,
- Communicating an organization's quality commitment,
- Communicating organizational quality policies, procedures, and requirements,
- Implementing efficient and effective ISO 9000 quality systems,
- Controlling and documenting key quality practices,
- Training employees in organizational quality requirements,
- Indicating specific compliance with the ISO 9000 standards,
- Illustrating how the company handles personnel training, engineering design changes, and other important operational information,
- Establishing a reference manual of approved, standardized, and accepted procedures and practices,
- Maintaining uniform and proceduralized practices,
- Maintaining capable and stabilized processes,
- Serving as a model for continuous improvement,
- Defining methods and requirements for training,
- Identifying management and line personnel responsible for ensuring that consistent standards are maintained,
- Communicating and emphasizing quality ISO 9000 commitment and compliance to the customer,
- Communicating ISO 9000 requirements to the organization and to other stakeholders,
- Ensuring there is uniform understanding and application of companywide quality policies,

- Identifying authorities and responsibilities for quality policy administration and practices,
- Proceduralizing the handling of recurring quality issues,
- Providing existing and new employees with a working guide to the company's quality beliefs and practices, and
- Establishing a reference point for auditing and correcting quality deficiencies.

# NUMBERING THE QUALITY MANUAL

Most commonly, quality documentation is organized following a one-to-one correspondence with ISO 9001/9002/9003 numbering, but other formats can be effective, too. Quality policies, procedures, and work instructions can be coded by clause, category, or sequence.

It's essential that quality documentation is accessible to the registrar's quality auditors and to internal users. The registrar's auditors use the manual as a roadmap to conduct the audit. First, the auditors evaluate the quality manual to ensure that it satisfies particular ISO 9000 clauses. This sometimes is called a *desk audit* or a *quality manual assessment*. Then the auditors use the manual as a guidepost when inquiring whether management and other personnel are familiar with and comply with ISO 9001/9002/9003.

In many existing quality manuals, quality documents are developed, issued, and filed whenever there is a new policy or procedure. The quality manual may have been developed when the company was founded and is revised as required. Policies and procedures are entered in the manual as they are developed, in chronological sequence. Personnel, manufacturing, purchasing, and quality policies and procedures may be filed in the same manual.

As long as the manual has only a few documents, this system works. Most employees know the procedures and consistently follow them. But as the organization grows, new employees may not know or follow them. Documentation then must be organized into functional areas and within each area organized in an alphanumeric outline or a decimal system.

The alphanumeric outline looks like the following:

I. A.
   B.
      1.
      2.
         a.
         b.

The decimal system follows the ISO 9001/9002/9003 organizational structure, as follows:

4.0. **Quality System Requirements**
    4.1. Management Responsibility
        4.1.1. Quality Policy
        4.1.2. Organization
            4.1.2.1. Responsibility and Authority

The decimal system is self-explanatory and is the most popular because it is easy to use. In this system, subcategories are created by adding a period to a section number. Documents can be found easily. Policies can be added, removed, revised, or submitted at any time. For example, a revision of Section 4.1.1, Quality Policy, can be made by adding a letter to the right of the section number—for example, 4.1.1A—to indicate the revision.

The ISO 9000 technical committee that developed and updates the ISO 9000 standards has published recommendations for structuring the quality manual. The recommendations in this book are consistent with this committee's recommendations. Key elements of the quality manual may include:

- Scope,
- History of the company,
- Description of the organization,
- Table of contents,
- Definitions and key concepts,
- Appendix,

- Binding and page numbering, and
- Lower-level or site quality manuals.

## SCOPE

The quality manual defines quality management, assurance, and control policies and activities for all company personnel. Where applicable, the quality manual also specifies activities and requirements for suppliers and subsuppliers.

Specifically, the quality manual defines policies describing how the quality program is designed to satisfy customers' requirements. Customer quality requirements are understood, specified, and communicated to all applicable operations. The goal is to ensure consistent and uniform products through maintaining stabilized and capable processes.

The quality manual defines how effective and efficient control is established by proceduralizing operations affecting quality and customer satisfaction.

The vice president or director of quality is the management representative with overall responsibility for the quality systems. Operational responsibility for quality rests with everyone in the organization.

## HISTORY OF THE COMPANY

A history of your company may help the customer understand your organization. The quality manual may be used as a sales document for sales personnel to show to prospective customers.

## DESCRIPTION OF THE ORGANIZATION

An organization chart is useful for the following reasons:

- It indicates who does what in the organization,
- The quality manual and the organization chart can be keyed to each other to indicate responsibilities and authorities for quality, and
- It indicates who is responsible for correcting a problem or conducting audits.

## Table of Contents

A table of contents lists the major categories and quality documentation that can be found in the manual. Each time a document is changed, the table of contents usually is modified to reflect the changes.

## Definitions and Key Concepts

Key concepts and definitions are included in the manual to ensure that standard ISO 9000 definitions and terms are used.

## Appendix

Peripheral documents that are not essential for communicating quality information are included in the appendix. These documents relate to quality but are not essential to controlling, measuring, or improving quality. Inserting them in the major sections of the manual confuses the user and makes the manual unwieldy. For example, the purchasing department may generate customer-supplier surveys or questionnaires that are essential to ensuring that purchased products conform to requirements. These documents are used to assess subcontracts as required in ISO 9001 4.6.2, Assessment of Sub-Contractors. The survey may be twenty or more pages, which would make the core quality manual needlessly bulky, but purchasing documents may be referenced in the purchasing procedures and placed in the procedural appendix.

## Binding and Page Numbering

Most paper quality manuals are bound in a three-ring loose-leaf binder. When sections, documents, or pages are revised, only pages need to be replaced.

Pages in the manual are not numbered sequentially. However, sections are numbered sequentially, and pages within a section are numbered sequentially. For example, purchasing would be the fourth section in the quality policy manual. The first page in this section is 4.1, and each following page is 4.2, 4.3, and so on.

Quality manuals may be used to communicate a quality commitment as a marketing tool. These manuals are printed on glossy paper and include background information about company officers, financial information, and products.

### LOWER-LEVEL OR SITE QUALITY MANUALS

The quality policy manual is an organizational quality document and is used by all business units, divisions, and plants in a large organization. The quality manual should be sufficiently generic to be usable in almost any culture and business environment.

*Quality procedural manuals*, on the other hand, can be specialized, tailored documents. They are division or plant specific because they detail procedures that may be entirely different from those used in other businesses. Many companies are now structured along business lines. One business unit may mine raw materials, while another processes these materials into ingots, which another business unit machines into finished products. Each business unit may be a separate business or plant that designs or produces a separate product. Each has its own quality manual.

# HOW TO DEVELOP QUALITY POLICIES AND PROCEDURES

ISO 9000 requires the development and implementation of documented quality systems, specifically a quality manual comprised of an organization's quality policies. To help organizations develop consistent quality manuals, an ISO technical committee is preparing a standard—ISO 10013, Guidelines for Developing Quality Manuals. The purpose of this document is to establish a uniform structure for organizations that are developing quality manuals. It should be emphasized that these are general recommendations for preparing the quality manual. They inevitably must be tailored to the specific needs to the user and the specific ISO 9001/9002/9003.

To begin with, each major department in the organization should be represented on the ISO 9000 committee. Whenever an operational or procedural change occurs, the committee determines whether a policy revision is required. If the committee determines that a change is needed, then the policy revision is formally evaluated, reviewed, and approved. The committee reviews all updates and revisions to ensure that there are no contradictions or inconsistencies in the documentation.

The quality department or the policy committee should review the quality documentation to ensure that it is current. The average life of an ISO 9000 policy manual is about five years because ISO 9001/9002/9003 is revised every four to five years. The manual should be thoroughly evaluated to ensure that it meets the intent and the letter of the latest revisions. If the manual is updated two or three years after the latest revision, then it quickly may become obsolete.

Lower-level documentation—procedures and work instructions—should be audited every six or twelve months. These documents reflect current operations, which may change and make the latest quality documentation out of date.

The following issues should be addressed in the quality documentation audit:

- Is the documentation
  - Current,
  - Complete,
  - Accurate,
  - Consistent,
  - Usable, and
  - Understandable?
- Have operations changed, and does quality documentation reflect the change?
- Do employees follow policies, procedures, and work instructions?
- Do employees have ownership in the policies?
- Are users and customers satisfied with the quality documentation?
- How can quality documentation be improved?
- Is quality documentation accessible?
- Is quality documentation approved and reviewed appropriately?

## QUALITY POLICIES, PROCEDURES, AND WORK INSTRUCTIONS

ISO 9000 documentation begins with the general and proceeds to the specific. Quality policies in the quality manual are generic; procedures are more specific and detailed. Quality policies describe in general terms the organization's required objectives and behavior. Quality procedures are more detailed and describe who does what, when, and where. Work procedures detail how it is done. Forms are used to document the result of quality activities.

There are twenty quality systems requirements in ISO 9001. Each quality procedure should reveal how the quality system requirement is implemented. The quality procedure section of this book illustrates each quality system requirement. The goal of this book is to have quality procedures that reflect how your work is done and to ensure that you meet ISO 9000 requirements.

Included here are examples of procedures for each quality system requirement, as well as detailed guides for developing and writing procedures for your specific operations. You can use these procedures to help you develop procedures in your own operation.

It's sometimes said that ISO 9000 implementation or registration is documentation intensive and extensive. Some people maintain that quality documentation has to be written for each quality activity, resulting in volumes of quality documentation detailing what, where, when, who, and why about everything in the organization. This misconception probably was initiated by an overzealous consultant.

The latest revisions of ISO 9001/9002/9003 require a quality manual—but the only acceptable ISO 9000 documentation trail is one that complies with specific ISO 9000 clauses.

## Developing the Quality Manual

The quality manual must first fit the organization—its processes and products. Then it must be usable and satisfy the needs of the users. Within these constraints, there is no one acceptable model of a quality manual, as indicated by the four quality manuals presented in this book. Even though the four quality manuals are from manufacturers, they are all a little different.

Quality policies should meet the needs of all department and business units of the organization. What's the best way to develop quality policies that represent the entire organization? One way is to have a committee drawn from the functional areas represent the organizational areas addressed by ISO 9000. This ensures that diverse views from throughout the organization are heard.

The committee should be large enough to represent all the major organizational areas affected as well as be small enough to be effective. Usually, the ISO

9000 quality committee has representatives from the human resources, quality, engineering, manufacturing, purchasing, and sales departments.

Senior management authorizes the development of the quality manual and usually assigns the development and coordination of the manual to an individual or to a group drawn from one or more functional areas.

The development group follows a logical process in developing, preparing, and obtaining approvals of the documents. The development process consists of the following steps:

- Identifying existing quality system policies and procedures,
- Understanding ISO 9001/9002/9003 requirements,
- Identifying internal quality systems that must comply with ISO 9001/9002/9003 requirements,
- Obtaining information about the existing quality systems from internal users,
- Developing and evaluating questionnaires on existing practices,
- Determining the format and structure of the quality manual,
- Classifying existing quality documents in terms of ISO 9000 compliance, and
- Developing quality policies and procedures required by ISO 9000.

The actual development and writing of the quality policies can be done by the coordination team, internal consultants, external consultants, or functional area employees. The function of the coordination team is to ensure accuracy, completeness, and continuity.

## APPROVAL OF THE QUALITY MANUAL

Prior to issuing the quality manual, its documents should be reviewed by all affected and responsible parties to ensure clarity, accuracy, suitability, and coherent structure. Internal stakeholders, customers, and suppliers should have the opportunity to assess the usability of the document. Final release should be authorized by the management level responsible for its implementation.

The quality manual should be accessible to all internal parties. Proper distribution, control, approval, and issuance can be ensured through serial copies of the documents.

Changes to the quality manual are incorporated and controlled by the quality department. The same review and approval process used in writing the quality manual also is used when incorporating changes. In some cases, the quality manual may contain sensitive information, in which case it is clearly identified as a controlled copy.

## How to Write Policies and Procedures

You may use two methods for developing quality policies. One method is to take off-the-shelf quality policies, possibly from this manual, implement them into an existing organization, and make little or no attempt to tailor them. If a company has no quality systems, then this approach is acceptable. As time goes by, these policies can be adapted to the existing organization, processes, and products. The preferred method of writing quality policies and procedures, however, is to write policies that have evolved from beliefs and practices.

## Standard Practices Becoming Policies

An organization may not have a quality manual or quality system in place, but customers still may seem to be satisfied, and products may seem to be defect free. The important word here is *seem*.

Standard operating practices and procedures become policies by default. Things are done this way because things always have been done this way or because someone was taught this way as the approved method. Ad hoc practices become unintentional policies. Management has done something one way, and this approach is communicated to the organization as the right and perhaps the only way to do something. The policy or decision is not questioned.

This may work at first, but problems may occur in the future under different situations, circumstances, or challenges. Employees may simply do what they think is right or seek clarifications, leading the company to operate under the exception principle.

## Communicating Policies

A quality policy manual by itself does little. Quality policies, procedures, and work instructions have to be used to be effective. Employees must know the policies, follow them, and apply them consistently. If they don't, then some method for clarification needs to be devised.

Management or the human resource department should train all employees by introducing, explaining, and demonstrating how to use quality documentation. Training is already an important quality system requirement. Training in quality can be through memos, lectures, on-job training, or other means.

In many companies, quality classes introduce quality concepts to new employees. Companywide quality policies are covered as well as job-specific quality requirements.

If a new procedure or work instruction has been developed and the organization is concerned about consistent implementation, then it may require users to return a signed acknowledgment that they read, understood, and will implement the new procedure. This may be especially necessary in new policy areas dealing with health, safety, and the environment. Federal and state regulatory agencies often conduct compliance audits and can levy heavy noncompliance fines.

## LEGAL REVIEW OF QUALITY DOCUMENTATION

Quality manuals may contain confidential or proprietary information. This is especially true of designs, bills of material, and work instructions. Process- and product-specific documentation is tightly controlled, with a master list or control list that indicates who has what type of quality documentation.

As quality documentation is adopted, published, and distributed, all existing copies of the manual should be updated. Users or holders of the manual are directed to remove and shred old pages and insert new pages. This requires self-discipline. People with heavy work loads often find that updating quality manuals may be the last thing that gets done.

Some quality documentation may be sent to those with a "need to know." If the information in the documentation is sufficiently sensitive, then the recipient may need military security clearances.

Should lawyers review quality documentation? In a large organization with its own counsel or legal department, it is a good idea to have a lawyer do a cursory review of quality and other documentation before it is released. This can be seen as a form of due diligence or damage control.

The house or outside counsel may review quality documentation for several reasons:

- To ensure that quality documentation complies with equal opportunity regulations, the Americans with Disabilities Act, and other regulations,

- To avoid implying or stating something that may be insensitive or prejudicial, and

- To ensure that no proprietary, sensitive, other documentation is inadvertently released.

A small company may not feel that quality documentation should be reviewed by a lawyer. But quality documentation is sent to suppliers, customers, regulatory agencies, and others. Moreover, federal and state regulatory agencies are developing burdensome and constantly changing rules in such areas as equal employment, affirmative action, health, safety, and other areas.

## COMMUNICATING POLICY AND PROCEDURAL CHANGES

ISO 9000 quality documentation may change the nature of an operation or process. If it does, then the organization should take steps to ensure that all employees are

- Informed of the change,

- Informed of the reason for the change,

- Notified when the change will take effect, and

- Notified who will assist in the implementation of the change.

System or process documentation or implementation changes can be announced through

- E-mail or a computerized bulletin board,

- A site bulletin board,

- Memos and newsletters, and

- Copies of the new procedure sent to all manual holders.

In general, the more specific the change, such as a process change or engineering revisions, the more instruction needed by the employee or team. A major process or engineering change can destabilize a process.

## It's People

Policies, procedures, and work instructions are not an end in themselves: in other words, they are not the final product. People are what count. The process of working with people to satisfy people—customers—is what is important.

Procedures shouldn't be seen as a mechanism for instilling fear, hindering creativity, or forestalling action. In today's team environment, quality documentation should be developed, positioned, and reinforced as a means for employees to control their own operations.

ISO 9000 quality documentation will be applied to a team environment. Sometimes, ISO 9000 quality documentation doesn't fit into this environment. The following are tips for integrating ISO quality documentation and procedures into a team work environment:

- Be aware of team members and work environment concerns. Team members respond best to fair and equitable policies and procedures.

- Have teams develop or even write ISO 9000 quality documentation. Team members respond best if they feel ownership and have input into the quality documentation.

- Be familiar with the culture and environment in which the quality documentation is developed. Organizational policies and procedures forced or imposed on a work area may not work.

- Use quality or human resource facilitators in developing site- or work-specific work instructions.

- Emphasize that quality documentation does not supplant good judgment and good decisions. Quality documentation serves as a guideline, but employees are empowered to do what's right.

- Develop the support of top area management in developing procedures and work instructions. If a general manager has been told to adopt ISO 9000 quality systems and write quality procedures, then he or she will impose them on the organization. If the general manager is unhappy, the people who have to develop and use the systems won't be happy.

- Be open about the ISO 9000 documentation and implementation process. Employees must own and maintain the quality systems after they have been developed.

# MANAGING QUALITY DOCUMENTATION

The purpose of proceduralizing operations is to reduce variation. Variation causes unstable operations. The secret of quality is to maintain consistency and uniformity.

Some believe that proceduralization stifles creativity by telling employees what to do in every circumstance. Procedures should serve as firm guidelines, but this doesn't mean that they must describe every element of a job. Some leeway must be allowed for specific situations.

The basic function of policies and procedures is to outline parameters or boundaries so that internal and external customers are satisfied with products and services. They also describe activities that enhance the quality of work life, satisfy regulations, and promote safety.

## QUALITY DOCUMENT ADMINISTRATION

Department and business unit heads are responsible for administering quality policies and procedures and ensuring that they are consistently followed.

The quality vice president or representative is responsible for establishing the policy committee and coordinating the development and deployment of quality policies. The quality representative will ensure that the quality manual, procedures, and work instructions are current, complete, and accurate.

The quality representative is responsible for coordinating the initial work of the committee, including calling meetings, assigning drafting responsibilities, auditing quality documentation, and revising documentation.

Representatives are also responsible for attending committee meetings, auditing documentation, communicating changes to respective departments, evaluating revisions, and apprising departments and the committee of changes, revisions, and additions.

Any employee can recommend changes, additions, deletions, and revisions to any quality documentation. The person must make the changes through the unit's quality policy committee representative, through the area supervisor, or through a quality documentation change request.

The policy committee discusses preparation of the quality documentation.

The chair then assigns responsibility for coordinating or preparing the draft of new or revised policies and procedures.

The chair or representative then coordinates preparation, review, and approval of the procedure draft with organizational administration, department heads, and others directly concerned with the subject area.

The policy committee provides final approval of all material to be included in the quality policy or procedures manuals.

## DISTRIBUTION OF QUALITY DOCUMENTATION

Quality manuals are assigned to positions and to locations. Manual holders are required to maintain assigned and current copies of quality documentation. The holders insert new pages when they are received and destroy superseded material.

All manuals remain on company property and are not for distribution. Holders are expected to return assigned copies on request, terminating employment, or transfer.

## MANAGING USING ISO 9000 DOCUMENTATION

Managing ISO quality requires a new focus in a team environment. At least superficially, ISO 9000 requirements don't seem like a good fit in work environments that emphasize team accountability and authority.

ISO 9000 documentation is customer-supplier contractual requirements. ISO 9001/9002/9003 are full of *shall* requirements. These must be developed carefully in a participatory work environment. Participatory work environments are characterized by self-managed, high-performance teams. The organization is flat. There are no middle managers. Teams are responsible and have the authority for their operations. Technical staff often assists teams and other work groups to do their jobs.

The critical question is how teams and more specifically team members feel about these *shall* requirements. ISO 9000 should be thoroughly explained to the entire organization. If senior management simply mandates ISO 9000 quality systems implementation, operations may be disrupted, possibly resulting in more scrap and increased rework.

ISO 9001/9002/9003 registration should be communicated as a customer or market requirement. If ISO 9000 registration is not pursued, then it may result in less work, which affects everyone. Using reason to communicate the urgency of registration is more effective than simply mandating a management-imposed dictate.

When ISO 9000 procedures are established for accountable work groups, these procedures and work instructions may at first seem threatening, especially if they seem to be imposed from above or from outside the organization. ISO 9000 quality systems should be integrated into existing procedures. Workers and teams should be involved throughout the process.

ISO 9000 registration requires quality systems to be implemented as well as fully documented. ISO 9000 procedures are centrally documented and maintained. Sometimes, this can create problems in organizations that resist bureaucracy and paperwork. In the ISO 9000 universe, more documentation results in more tasks as activities are performed and recorded. ISO 9000 documentation creates a living system. Any change in a process or system is reflected in changes to the documentation.

As paperwork snowballs, as more operations are proceduralized, there arises the question of what type of quality system should be implemented—paperwork, computerized, or a combination of both. For small companies a paper-based system is adequate. Paper can be accessed easily, and a small number of paper quality systems are manageable. However, in larger companies a computer may be necessary to manage the documentation. Documentation must be kept current, complete, and be usable. Computerization of documentation is difficult. It is expensive because people must be trained, computers purchased, software purchased, and new procedures developed.

## TIPS FOR DEVELOPING THE QUALITY MANUAL

You can use the following tips to develop your own ISO 9000 quality document:

- *Make it comprehensive.* The quality manual addresses all the applicable ISO 9000 quality system requirements.

- *Make it understandable.* The quality manual is written simply and directly so that most employees understand and follow its message.

- *Make it usable.* The manual can be used as a quality guide for creating and helping maintain registration.

- *Keep it short and simple.* Notice that the four examples of quality manuals in this book are about fifteen to twenty pages long. Many documentation people still believe that the manual should be all inclusive. As a rule, a quality manual ten to forty pages long can still address the requirements of ISO 9001/9002/9003 and be tailored to your organization.

- *Select a template.* Several acceptable formats can be followed for developing the quality manual. There is no one best method. The important point is to follow a consistent format in terms of writing, words, quality concepts, and clause numbering.

- *Make it appealing.* Quality manuals are sometimes used as sales documents with existing or prospective customers. If you're going to use yours as a sales document, then it should be packaged appropriately in heavy glossy paper with perhaps four-color pictures.

- *Make it grammatically correct.* Especially if this document is being used as a sales piece, the quality manual should be grammatically correct. What image will you convey if your manual says, "Quality processes is . . . ?"

- *Ensure that there is a master copy.* A master copy of all quality documentation should be filed in the quality department. Although the quality manual won't change often, quality procedures, work instructions, drawings, bills of material, specifications may change frequently. A central clearing office ensures that document changes are consistently incorporated into the document and that the latest revisions are communicated to all document holders.

- *Ensure that there is a one-to-one mapping between ISO 9001/9002/9003 and the quality manual.* The registrar's quality auditor will first evaluate you in terms of addressing the ISO 9001/9002/9003 requirements. This is sometimes called a *quality manual assessment* or *desk audit*. If the quality manual is organized like the ISO 9000 standard, the auditor will have a much easier time understanding your quality systems.

- *Understand ISO 9001/9002/9003 quality system requirements.* This will allow you to develop quality documentation that fits your company.

- *Tailor your manual to your company.* The quality manual should follow the ISO 9001/9002/9003 as closely as possible. Sometimes, a company will adopt ISO 9001/9002/9003 language verbatim. You don't have to go this far. Follow the sample quality manuals in this book, and paraphrase and tailor them to your specific operations, products, or processes.

- *Revise and rewrite.* The quality manual will require revisions until it is adopted. Three or more revisions may be required until it is fully accepted. The iterative development process is important for developing organizational buy-in.

- *Use your quality manual as your foundation document.* All quality documentation is tiered. At the top of the hierarchy is the quality manual, and then procedures, work instructions, and forms fill out the rest of the pyramid. Tie each level to the next if possible.

- *Ensure buy-in into the quality manual.* The quality manual is a companywide policy document.

- *Be clear, accurate, and comprehensive.* Everyone's goal is to have a clear and accurate quality manual. During the review and revision process, however, the document may become dense, reflecting everyone's requirements. Make sure one editor incorporates everyone's comments and maintains consistency of language and style.

- *Develop an understandable and usable document.* The quality manual is a companywide quality document. It should be understandable. Avoid terms that are too elaborate, awkward, complex, or unorthodox.

- *Use common ISO 9000 terms and concepts.* ISO 9000 is an international set of quality standards. The ISO 9000 technical committee, which was commissioned to write and update the standards, has spent much time obtaining consensus on common quality terms and concepts. ISO 8402 defines these quality terms. Use these terms when writing your quality documentation.

- *Use neutral language.* The language in quality documentation is now gender neutral. Gender neutral language does not offend or discriminate. Until a few years ago, it was common to say that *he* will do something. Now, the more common expression is *he or she* or even better *person*.

- *Strive for a moderate length.* Quality policies should communicate essential information about the organization's position on a topic. Quality procedures should communicate the proper methods for implementing policies. Quality work instructions should communicate how to perform a specific task. Quality forms should be usable by the entire organization.

- *Use the KISS principle.* The KISS (Keep It Short and Simple) principle applies to writing quality documentation. Ideas are expressed best when they are concise, clear, and to the point. The drawback of overprecision is that it can lead to confusion, limit creativity, or limit initiative.

## LACK OF QUALITY DOCUMENTATION

The consequences of missing, conflicting, or misunderstanding policies, procedures, and work instructions can be confusion and even harm. Sending deficient products to customers can result in a possible recall. Variation among plants, departments, teams, methods, and people can result in contradictory practices and decisions.

Written quality documentation can prevent variation, confusion, chaos, and litigation. Everyone wants to do a job right. But what is right? Is right what the employee thinks, what the supervisor believes, or what the customer wants or expects? One of the major objectives of quality documentation is to define what is right for the organization and its stakeholders.

In some organizations employees are felt to be capable of determining what is right, and doing right is a simple, responsible, individual, or group decision. When problems arise, the person or team—guided by instinct, good will, skills, and knowledge—will do what it feels is right or correct for the moment. Trouble may develop, however, if the person or team does not anticipate all developments, understand upstream or downstream process requirements, have sufficient background knowledge, or understand all stakeholder requirements. Written, consensual quality documentation should serve as the roadmap and milestones for quality activities.

## Quality Documentation Challenges

If quality policies exist, they should be used and adhered to. However, this may not be the case for several reasons:

- Policies may not have been distributed to all managers or operating groups,
- Teams may not be using them because they have not been updated,
- New employees have not been introduced to the policies, procedures, or work instructions,
- In a culturally diverse workplace, new employees may not be able to read or understand the procedures and work instructions,
- Policies have not been updated in a long time,
- Employees are not aware of the existence of the work instructions,
- Quality policies may be contradictory, and
- Departments follow different practices than those spelled out in quality documentation.

## Seek Expert Advice

The quality policies manual and other quality documentation provided in this book are generic. They are supplied as examples of common ISO 9000 quality documentation, but they have to be tailored to your specific requirements. Cut and paste these documents to come up with a document that meets your requirements. If you still have questions, then seek the advice of a consultant, join a user's group, or attend an ISO 9000 seminar.

# QUALITY DOCUMENTATION

Quality documentation is found in three major sections in this book:

- Quality manuals, level I documentation,
- Quality procedures, level II documentation, and
- Quality forms, level IV documentation

ISO 9000 requires a quality manual and establishing and maintaining quality system procedures. Specifically, ISO 9001 requires that a "supplier shall prepare a quality manual covering the requirements of this American National Standard."[1] ISO 9001 also states that the "quality manual shall include or make reference to the quality system procedures and outline the structure of the documentation used in the quality system."[2]

Why didn't I add a section of examples of work instructions, Level III documentation, since there is a section of quality forms? Examples of quality forms are presented to illustrate how quality forms may be tied to specific quality procedures. However, work instructions are generic documents detailing how a job function should be performed. These documents are not specifically required by ISO 9000.

## SAMPLE QUALITY MANUALS

Four sample quality manuals are presented in this book. Each is a little different. The first quality manual is more detailed and rigorous reflecting the quality requirements of a large organization. In some respects, the first quality manual surpasses the specific requirements of ISO 9001. This organization has very extensive and intensive quality systems.

Each succeeding manual is less detailed. However, each quality manual meets

---

[1] ANSI/ASQC Q9001–1994, "Quality Systems—Model for Quality Assurance in Design, Development, Production, Installation, and Servicing," p. 2.

[2] ANSI/ASQC Q9001–1994, "Quality Systems—Model for Quality Assurance in Design, Development, Production, Installation, and Servicing," p. 2.

the requirements of ISO 9001. An exception, is sample Quality Manual #3, which illustrates compliance to ISO 9002. Note that the scope of ISO 9002 does not include design control. Also, Section 19, Servicing, is not shown because the company is not required by the customer to service its products.

You'll notice that the quality manuals are very different from each other. Sample quality manuals #3 and #4 describe compliance to the quality system requirements in less detail. That's acceptable. Each quality manual is tailored to fit the needs of the organization and its stakeholders. ISO 9000 quality systems requirements may be added or deleted depending on your organizational requirements, contractual needs, and stakeholder expectations.

ISO 9001 specifically states that "it is not the purpose of these American National Standards to enforce uniformity of quality systems."[3] ISO 9001/9002/9003 specify generic quality system documentation requirements that are designed to fulfill an organization's process, product, and service requirements and practices.

## SAMPLE QUALITY PROCEDURES

The sample quality procedures are organized by ISO 9001 quality system requirements. They are used to illustrate specific responses with the intent of complying with ISO 9001 requirements. Most of the procedures are one page in length and follow a consistent format of "purpose," "scope," and "procedure."

A policy and a procedure may look very similar. The policy or procedure can be computerized or be in paper form. The procedure can be organized in almost any fashion depending on user requirements. However, it is common practice for a procedure to contain the following:

- The purpose of the procedure,
- The scope or areas or activities that are affected by the procedure,
- What activity or activities will be accomplished,
- Who (a team or an individual) will accomplish the activity or action,
- When the activity will be completed,
- How the activity will be accomplished,

---

[3] ANSI/ASQC Q9001–1994, "Quality Systems—Model for Quality Assurance in Design, Development, Production, Installation, and Servicing," p. vii.

- What equipment is required to accomplish the activity, and

- How the results of the activity will be documented, controlled, or monitored.

Quality procedures also provide the following benefits:

- Consistency, continuity, and understanding within the organization,

- Figures or graphs that communicate details better than narrative descriptions, and

- Help supervisors in achieving consistent application of procedures.

The procedures in this book are prepared specifically for small and medium-sized businesses pursuing ISO 9001/9002/9003 registration. The contents are based on the current requirements of ISO 9000, which should be obtained and studied before you proceed with your own quality documentation.

Although you can cut and paste your quality manual, procedures are more detailed and must be tailored to your specific operations.

## SAMPLE QUALITY FORMS

The sample quality forms are arranged alphabetically by title. They represent the basic forms used to comply with generic ISO 9000 quality systems. The forms can be used with different quality system requirements. For example, the Corrective Action Request (CAR) form can be used with the Corrective Action Request and Internal Quality Audit quality system requirements.

# SAMPLE QUALITY MANUALS

# SAMPLE QUALITY MANUAL 1

## ISO 9001: 4.1
### MANAGEMENT RESPONSIBILITY

1.0 **QUALITY POLICY.** QM anticipates and exceeds customer's requirements and expectations through cost-competitive quality products and services that are delivered on time, every time.

1.1 QM's executive management is committed to total customer satisfaction through cost-competitive quality products and services. Senior management presents quarterly updates of new companywide quality policies and procedures.

2.0 **ORGANIZATION.** QM's quality organization personnel have the authority and responsibility to maintain, implement, and update QM's quality system. This includes
- Defining customer quality requirements,
- Specifying system, process, and product quality requirements,
- Initiating corrective action to prevent nonconformances,
- Identifying and recording nonconformances through organizational channels,
- Initiating changes to eliminate symptoms and root causes, and
- Verifying the effectiveness of corrective action.

2.1 All QM personnel are responsible for verifying system and product compliance to QM policies and procedures. Quality systems auditing is conducted in all company operations by trained, independent, and objective individuals.

2.2 QM has a corporate executive responsible for maintaining and ensuring ISO 9001 quality system registration, for conducting corporate internal quality audits, for ensuring improvement of internal quality systems, for liaising with external parties concerning the organization's quality systems and for reporting on the performance of internal quality systems. The corporate quality executive is Jane Smith. The business unit representative is the quality vice president. The plant representative is the quality assurance manager.

3.0 **MANAGEMENT REVIEW OF QUALITY SYSTEMS.** QM's quality policies, procedures, and overall quality system are periodically reviewed by executive management and audited by business-unit and plant-designated personnel.

3.1 The overall total quality management system is audited and reviewed at the corporate, business-unit, and plant levels at least once a year. The head of quality at each organizational level is responsible for the audit. The review covers
- Complete, current, and accurate specifications,
- Application of procedures,
- Quality manual completeness, and
- Corrective action effectiveness.

Executive management reviews quality strategic plans, tactical plans, accountabilities, policies, procedures, and benchmarks to improve operational effectiveness, efficiency, and economy. Records of all reviews and audits are maintained at the QM corporate quality office.

# ISO 9001: 4.2
## QUALITY SYSTEM

1.0 **GENERAL QUALITY SYSTEM.** QM maintains organizational, personnel, and quality systems to ensure external and internal customer satisfaction through cost-competitive quality products and services.

1.1 QM maintains total quality management systems to ensure internal and external customer satisfaction in its products and services.

1.2 ISO 9001 forms the foundation and structure of all QM's quality systems. QM's corporate and business-unit quality manuals define current policies and procedures for complying with the latest ISO 9001 revision. Each site has its own specific quality documentation, including policies and work instructions detailing the control and management of quality.

1.3 QM's quality systems are certified and registered by Quality Science Registrars. QM notifies the registrar of significant quality system changes. The quality officer at the appropriate organizational level is responsible for notifying the registrar of quality system changes.

2.0 **QUALITY SYSTEMS DOCUMENTATION.** Quality systems documentation includes quality policies, procedures, work instructions, and other documentation. ISO 9001 quality policies and procedures are incorporated into the corporate and business-unit quality manuals.

2.1 Quality manual numbering corresponds to ISO 9001 clauses.

3.0 **QUALITY PLAN.** QM has developed quality plans to ensure operational consistency and prevent nonconformances. Quality analysis planning involves all operational personnel, including professional, administrative, service, and production. The goal of quality planning is to ensure customer satisfaction through the delivery of quality products and services. Quality plans are developed for each new contract, new product, modified product, or process change. Quality plans include but are not limited by the following:

- Controlling and improving quality through the acquisition of new products, processes, equipment, people, or other resources,
- Identifying and defining the quality process and product characteristics,
- Ensuring the compatibility of design, manufacturing, purchasing, test, and delivery procedures and documentation,
- Updating quality control processes and procedures to maintain and improve quality,
- Identifying measurement or process capability requirements that surpass ability of equipment,
- Identifying quality controls and suitable verification throughout the product-development, purchasing, manufacturing, and delivery cycles, and
- Maintaining and updating required quality documentation.

4.0 **QUALITY RECORDS.** Quality documentation is maintained according to quality procedures.

5.0 **RESPONSIBILITY.** The chief quality officer of the operational unit is responsible for ensuring that quality procedures are monitored and improved. All employees are responsible for following quality procedures and for continuous, measurable improvement.

5.1 QM quality management reviews quality policies, systems, procedures, and documentation. Quality audits and reviews focus on operational efficiency, effectiveness, and economy.

## ISO 9001: 4.3
## CONTRACT REVIEW

1.0 **CONTRACT REQUIREMENTS.** Customer documentation tenders, offers, and contracts are reviewed prior to acceptance to ensure that customer requirements are defined and understood. This applies to all types of contract orders, both written and verbal. The QM quality organization identifies internal parties who should review new contracts. Before acceptance, all internal parties review and approve new contract requirements. The following contractual quality documentation is thoroughly reviewed prior to acceptance:
- Purchase orders,
- Product and process specifications,
- Quality plans,
- Control and capability requirements,
- Verbal offers and instructions, and
- Special instructions or requirements.

2.0 **CUSTOMER CONTRACT REVIEW.** New or modified product contracts are reviewed to ensure that
- New requirements are defined and understood,
- New requirements can be complied with, and
- New requirements are properly reviewed by all parties.

3.0 **NEW PRODUCT DEVELOPMENT.** Customer satisfaction, defect prevention, and continuous improvement are key elements of new product development.

4.0 **CAPABILITIES.** Existing and new product contracts are evaluated in terms of QM's ability to satisfy all customer requirements. Equipment, environment personnel, engineering, manufacturing, methods, tooling, and other systems are also evaluated.

5.0 **RECORDS.** Contract review records are maintained and accessible to all QM parties. External party review must be approved by QM management.

# ISO 9001: 4.4
## DESIGN CONTROL

1.0 **DESIGN DEVELOPMENT AND PLANNING.** Designs are controlled, documented, and planned throughout product development to ensure that specified requirements are satisfied. Design output and input variables are identified, controlled, monitored, measured, and documented throughout product development.

1.1 Product design and verification activities are planned by and assigned to quality representatives for review. Critical individuals for reviewing designs are identified. Design changes are documented and reviewed by designated individuals.

1.2 Design control information is documented, communicated, and reviewed throughout product development.

2.0 **DESIGN INPUT.** Product requirements are identified and documented. Groups with specific expertise that can contribute are identified. Regulatory, safety, and health requirements are identified and reviewed for adequacy and compliance. Conflicting requirements are resolved by QM project and product managers. Design input also considers the results of previous contract reviews.

3.0 **DESIGN OUTPUT.** Design output is documented in terms of satisfying customer requirements by
- Meeting design input requirements,
- Defining process and product requirements,
- Containing acceptance criteria,
- Conforming to industry requirements and government regulations, and
- Classifying and prioritizing product attributes that deal with safety, health, consumer protection, or environmental conditions.

4.0 **DESIGN VERIFICATION.** Designs are planned, documented, and verified throughout the product-development process. Design verification involves the following:
- Holding design reviews,
- Conducting reliability testing,
- Analyzing design calculations,
- Comparing designs against competitors' products,
- Conducting independent analysis,
- Testing products in different environments,

- Reviewing all design-related documents, and
- Reviewing safety and health issues.

5.0 **DESIGN REVIEW.** Formal documented reviews of design criteria and results are planned, and conducted throughout the product development process.

6.0 **DESIGN CHANGES.** Design modifications, changes, or revisions are monitored, controlled, verified, validated, and documented through the engineering change order (ECO) system. The ECO system is close-looped so that it identifies changes, permits reviews of the changes, and secures approvals. Authorized personnel sign off on all design changes.

## ISO 9001: 4.5
## DOCUMENT AND DATA CONTROL

1.0 **APPROVAL AND ISSUE.** Quality systems are documented and controlled. Control involves the issue, approval, review, distribution, and modification of quality documents and data.

1.1 ISO 9000 and customer documents and data are available at appropriate operational locations involving quality systems. If necessary, customer, regulatory, and other critical documents and data are available at the business unit's or corporate quality office.

2.0 **MODIFICATIONS.** Document and data changes are reviewed and approved by the same functional groups and preferably by the same personnel who initially approved the documentation. A master list of approved changes to quality documentation is maintained and controlled by the site quality personnel, who ensure that

- Quality documentation and data are readily available to all site personnel,
- Obsolete documents are removed from manuals, computers, and other locations, and
- Obsolete regulatory, health, or safety-related documents are maintained if required by QM's legal department.

# ISO 9001: 4.6
## PURCHASING

1.0 **SELECTION AND EVALUATION OF SUPPLIERS.** Suppliers of products and services are selected, monitored, and improved through specified requirements involving quality, delivery, service, and cost.

1.1 Suppliers are selected and evaluated based on the following criteria:
- Past history,
- Process control site audit,
- Process control and capability,
- Self-assessment,
- Product inspection and testing,
- Performance history, and
- Reliability, maintainability, and other testing.

1.2 Each business unit maintains and evaluates records of supplier performance.

2.0 **PURCHASING DATA AND DOCUMENTATION.** Purchasing information is documented, current, complete, and accurate.

2.1 All purchasing and customer documentation is retained, including
- Purchase order,
- Engineering prints,
- Supplier evaluation forms, and
- Product test data.

2.2 QM quality representatives review and approve all customer and supplier documentation throughout the product-development and product life cycles.

2.3 Customer requirements and expectations are fully described in documentation, including
- Type, number, level, and other data of required materials,
- Type of services,
- Acceptance levels,
- Delivery requirements,
- Costs,
- Performance requirements,
- Engineering and manufacturing process, and
- Corrective actions.

2.4 QM retains the right to audit on-site supplier processes, testing, or other supplier activities. The supplier is still responsible for satisfying contract requirements and for approving acceptable products.

## ISO 9000: 4.7
### CONTROL OF CUSTOMER-SUPPLIED PRODUCT

1.0 **PROCEDURES.** Procedures are established for specifying, identifying, handling, transporting, and storing purchased materials.

1.1 Qualified stores' personnel identify, count, and verify that supplied materials conform to contract and quality requirements. Conforming and nonconforming materials are segregated, stored, handled, and tagged according to procedures.

1.2 Purchased materials are stored, handled, and transported according to approved procedures and industry standards.

2.0 **LOST, DAMAGED, OR UNSUITABLE MATERIALS.** Lost, damaged, or unsuitable materials are documented and reported to the customer.

3.0 **RESPONSIBILITY.** Responsibility for meeting QM's requirements still rests with the supplier.

## ISO 9001: 4.8
### PRODUCT IDENTIFICATION AND TRACEABILITY

1.0 **MATERIAL AND PRODUCT IDENTIFICATION.** Procedures are established and maintained to identify and document materials and products throughout the product-development and product life cycles.

2.0 **TRACEABILITY.** In-house and purchased materials are traced through the product-development and product life cycles. Traceability also extends to delivery and installation. If required by contract, QM can identify individual batches, shipments, or products.

## ISO 9001: 4.9
### PROCESS CONTROL

1.0 **GENERAL PROCESSES.** All major organizational processes are controlled. If applicable, processes are in control and capable.

1.1 Process control may include documented procedures, trained employees, statistically controlled machinery, process approval, workmanship criteria, installation and servicing equipment, monitored environments, and calibrated equipment. Procedure and work instructions are developed for each job. Each employee understands his or her responsibilities. Quality systems are evaluated periodically to ensure that they are current, accurate, and complete. Internal customer satisfaction is also monitored.

2.0 **SPECIAL PROCESSES.** Special processes are those that are operator dependent.

2.1 Special processes are monitored and controlled.

2.2 Process control requirements are defined for critical process parameters and product characteristics.

2.3 Outputs from special processes are monitored to ensure that they comply with specifications, procedures, and instructions.

2.4 Records are maintained and available for special processes, equipment, and personnel.

2.5 Requirements for certifying any special process operations are also specified.

## ISO 9001: 4.10
### INSPECTION AND TESTING

1.0 **RECEIVING INSPECTION AND TESTING.** Materials and products are inspected according to documented procedures to ensure conformance to specifications. Required inspection and testing are detailed in quality plans.

1.1 Receiving inspection ensures that incoming materials conform to quality specifications. If materials cannot or are not inspected, then certifications of compliance may be required from the supplier. Materials from certified suppliers are not inspected.

1.2 The quality organization is responsible for generating and controlling inspection reports and supplier quality documentation.

1.3 First-item sample products from suppliers are evaluated by the quality and engineering departments. Results are communicated to the purchasing department for supplier approval. First-item samples must be received and evaluated prior to production. First-item samples are required for new products, modifications of existing products, new suppliers, or new processes. The engineering, quality, manufacturing, and purchasing departments must sign off on the first-item samples. On acceptance, an approval document is generated with test results.

Purchasing is responsible for communicating approval to the supplier. If the sample is rejected, all documentation is sent to purchasing, which communicates the reasons for the rejection and alternatives to the supplier.

1.4 If material is urgently required, engineering, quality, manufacturing, and purchasing jointly approve the waiver.

2.0 **IN-PROCESS INSPECTION AND TESTING.** In-process testing and inspection stations are identified on a flow chart, quality plan, or similar document. Supplementary documentation identifies type of inspection, product characteristics, inspection methods, inspection levels, Acceptable Quality Levels (AQLs), and inspection equipment.

3.0 **FINAL INSPECTION AND TESTING.** Final testing and inspection stations are identified on a flow chart, quality plan, or similar document. Supplementary documentation identifies type of inspection, product characteristics, inspection methods, inspection levels, AQLs, and inspection equipment.

4.0 **INSPECTION AND TEST RECORDS.** Inspection and test records are maintained and indicate conformance. The quality plan details all specified inspection and tests, locations, results, and disposition of products.

# ISO 9001: 4.11
## CONTROL OF INSPECTION, MEASURING, AND TEST EQUIPMENT

1.0 **GENERAL REQUIREMENTS.** During product development, key product characteristics are identified on engineering prints or similar documents. Inspection, measuring, and test equipment is identified to measure the previously indicated product characteristic accurately and precisely. All critical and major inspection, measuring, and test equipment calibration processes are controlled, including type of equipment, unique identification, location, frequency of check, check method, verification criteria, and corrective action results. Inspection, measurement, and test equipment is calibrated for precision and accuracy at documented prescribed intervals. Calibration status is recorded on gauges and on quality documentation. Test software is also controlled to determine product conformance. In-house reference calibration is conducted in controlled conditions. Inspection, measurement, and test are all proceduralized. Internal reference gauges and external calibration service are transferable to NIST (National Institute for Standards and Technology).

2.0 **RESPONSIBILITIES.** Responsibilities for inspection, measurement, and testing are detailed. All organizational personnel are responsible for checking and ensuring accurate and precise measurement equipment. Measurement equipment is stored, handled, and secured according to procedures.

3.0 **SPECIFIC REQUIREMENTS.** Specific requirements for measurement equipment are that
- Product and process measurements are identified,
- Measuring equipment is properly identified,
- Location, calibration date, calibration frequency, authority, and other criteria are documented,
- Damaged or uncalibrated equipment is segregated,
- Calibration processes are evaluated,
- Calibration records are maintained,
- Previous calibration accuracy is validated if necessary,
- Environmental conditions are checked, and
- Handling, storage, and security of measuring equipment are checked.

## ISO 9001: 4.12
### INSPECTION AND TEST STATUS

1.0. **IDENTIFICATION.** Inspection and test status of the product are identified throughout production. Nonconforming products are properly tagged and segregated. Conforming products are released to the next production step only if identification indicates proper release status. Identification must follow procedures and may include tags, labels, or marks.

2.0. **AUTHORITY.** Release authority for conforming products is identified on products, lots, or shipments.

## ISO 9001: 4.13
### CONTROL OF NONCONFORMING PRODUCT

1.0. **CONTROL OF NONCONFORMING MATERIAL AND PRODUCTS.** Nonconforming products are identified, evaluated, segregated, and disposed of according to procedures. Quality procedures detail responsibility and authority for determining the cause and disposing of nonconforming material and products.

2.0. **REVIEW AND INSPECTION.** Nonconforming materials are reviewed according to procedures. They may be
- Scrapped,
- Reworked,
- Used as is,
- Returned to supplier, or
- Regraded.

3.0 **RETENTION OR DISPOSAL.** Nonconforming products are retained or disposed of according to procedures. Repaired or reworked products are reinspected according to inspection procedures. Records are maintained of any action dealing with materials.

# ISO 9001: 4.14
## CORRECTIVE AND PREVENTIVE ACTION

1.0. **GENERAL PURPOSE.** Corrective and preventive actions are planned and documented. Corrective action focuses on eliminating the symptom and the root cause. Preventive action focuses on eliminating occurrences and recurrences.

2.0. **CORRECTIVE ACTION.** Nonconformances, flaws, or deficiencies are prioritized, and the most significant are analyzed and eliminated first. Some of the analysis tools used are cost of quality, statistical process control (SPC), customer complaints, and inspection results. Corrective action also involves
- Analyzing customer complaints,
- Analyzing product nonconformances,
- Investigating the cause of the above nonconformances,
- Determining the cause of corrective actions, and
- Applying controls to prevent recurrence.

3.0. **PREVENTIVE ACTION.** The goal of preventive action is to prevent occurrences and recurrences of nonconformances and deficiencies. The results of preventive action are investigated to ensure that problems do not recur. Preventive action also involves
- Analyzing data and information to detect and analyze potential causes of nonconformances,

- Developing a plan to prevent occurrences and recurrences or nonconformances,
- Initiating preventive action, and
- Evaluating the effectiveness of preventive action.

4.0. **DOCUMENTATION AND RECORDS.** Corrective action from initiation to result is documented properly.

## ISO 9001: 4.15
## HANDLING, STORAGE, PACKAGING, PRESERVATION, AND DELIVERY

1.0. **GENERAL PROCEDURES.** Production materials are identified so there is an audit trail from incoming material to customer delivery or to final disposition. Procedures are developed for handling, storing, packaging, and delivering materials.

2.0. **HANDLING.** Handling procedures ensure that materials are not damaged through the production cycle. Procedures and drawings prescribe proper containers. Procedures also detail special handling requirements.

3.0. **STORAGE.** Storage procedures ensure that materials are not damaged through the production cycle. Storage procedures instruct personnel on maintaining proper environmental conditions in designated storage areas or stock rooms.

4.0. **PACKAGING.** Packaging procedures ensure that materials are not damaged throughout the production cycle. Packaging is designed to meet customer requirements, type of transportation, product, cost, and other factors.

5.0. **PRESERVATION.** Preservation procedures detail appropriate methods for ensuring products continue to conform to requirements.

6.0. **DELIVERY.** Delivery procedures ensure that materials are not damaged during internal or external transit. If delivery misuses or abuses the product, proper packaging can ensure that materials still conform to requirements.

## ISO 9001: 4.16
### CONTROL OF QUALITY RECORDS

1.0. **GENERAL REQUIREMENTS.** Quality records are generated and maintained throughout the organization for all critical activities and functions, including identification, collecting, indexing, accessing, filing, maintaining, and disposing of quality records. Quality records can be retrieved easily and are available to all personnel. Quality records are identifiable, accurate, complete, and current. Quality records are traceable and auditable to processes, products, and results.

2.0. **RECORDS TYPES.** Many types of quality records are retained, including
- Specifications,
- Quality costs,
- Supplier quality,
- Inspection and measurement,
- Internal audits,
- Design review,
- Customer complaints,
- Process quality,
- Product performance,
- Corrective action, and
- Audit results.

3.0. **RETENTION.** Quality records are retained according to specific requirements in procedures and policies. Records are available for review by the customer. Quality records may be stored in electronic or hard media.

## ISO 9001: 4.17
### INTERNAL QUALITY AUDITS

1.0. **AUDIT SCHEDULE.** Quality audits are conducted to verify quality activities, quality planning compliance, and quality system effectiveness. Quality audits are prioritized based on importance, cost, and internal requirements.

2.0. **AUDIT-SPECIFIC REQUIREMENTS.** Area quality organizations are responsible for planning, conducting, and reporting audit results. Quality audits are conducted by independent, trained, and qualified personnel.

Audits follow documented procedures. All organizational quality processes, systems, and products are audited.

- 3.0. **RESULTS.** Audit reports are distributed to the specified people defined in the procedures. Audited areas may be reaudited to evaluate efficiency, effectiveness, and economy of corrective action. Follow-up audits may be conducted to verify and record the effectiveness of correction action.
- 3.1. The entire organization, the business units, and the plants are audited yearly to determine compliance with policies and procedures.

## ISO 9001: 4.18
### TRAINING

- 1.0. **GENERAL REQUIREMENTS.** All employees are trained to do their jobs properly so that internal and ultimately external customers are satisfied. Job requirements for performing the required quality work are spelled out.
- 2.0. **QUALITY TRAINING.** Quality is an essential element of the training and development of new and existing employees. Training efforts are periodically evaluated and updated. Critical elements of quality training are
    - External and internal customer satisfaction,
    - Customer satisfaction through total quality management,
    - Prevention and continuous improvement to keep up with changing customer expectations,
    - Establishment of benchmarks and measurement of progress, and
    - Acknowledgment that suppliers are important partners in the improvement process.
- 3.0. **RESPONSIBILITIES.** Operational and functional area heads are responsible for ensuring that training and development objectives are attained and documented.
- 4.0. **RECORDS.** Training records are maintained for all employees.
- 5.0. **TRAINING PROGRAMS.** Quality training is industry, company, process, and product specific.

## ISO 9001: 4.19
### SERVICING

1.0. **GENERAL REQUIREMENTS.** Service process, systems, and documentation properly address service requirements. After-sales service is documented so that customer requirements are satisfied. Internal and external customers are surveyed to determine customer satisfaction.

2.0. **RESPONSIBILITIES.** Customer service accountabilities are defined for all appropriate personnel.

3.0. **RECORDS.** Service records—including survey results, failure modes, costs, and studies—are maintained and periodically assessed.

## ISO 9001: 4.20
### STATISTICAL TECHNIQUES

1.0. **GENERAL REQUIREMENTS.** Statistical techniques are established for appropriate business processes. Personnel are trained in statistical prevention. Records are maintained to record the result of statistical analysis and to pursue continuous improvement.

2.0. **SAMPLING PLANS.** Sampling and inspection plans reflect the supplier's process capabilities, type of products, product characteristics, costs, and risks.

3.0. **TECHNIQUES.** The list of statistical techniques includes but is not limited to the following:
- Statistical process control (SPC),
- Taguchi methods,
- Histograms,
- Reliability calculations,
- Engineering calculations, and
- Sampling.

4.0. **APPLICATIONS.** Statistical analysis is used in the following:
- Reliability testing,
- Production processes,
- Engineering product development,
- Market analysis,
- Continuous improvement, and
- Customer satisfaction.

# SAMPLE QUALITY MANUAL 2

## 4.1 MANAGEMENT RESPONSIBILITY

*Purpose*

The purpose of this clause is to define the organization's quality policy, organization, authorities, responsibilities, executive representative, management review, and verification personnel.

*Policy*

Each organizational employee is responsible for ensuring that customers' requirements, expectations, and needs are consistently met each and every time. Quality is everyone's responsibility. Executive management is responsible for defining and documenting quality policies and objectives. Executive management is responsible for ensuring that training, equipment, and other resources are available for satisfying customer requirements and expectations. These policy statements are understood, operationalized, and maintained throughout the organization. Policy statement revisions are developed, discussed, and agreed on by all organizational members. Revisions are incorporated immediately into the manual.

Executive management authorities, responsibilities, and interrelationships are listed in an organizational chart. The major organizational areas include quality, human resources, sales/marketing, engineering, purchasing, manufacturing and production, and finance.

✤ ✤ ✤

The quality department is responsible for maintaining the job descriptions and skill inventories of all employees. The quality department is also responsible for conducting internal and external quality audits of training, records maintenance, and resource availability. The quality assurance department within the quality department is responsible for quality improvement, testing, inspection, and equipment calibration. Special job requirements are clearly defined and filed in the human resources department. Quality requirements are specified for each position, and each person is sufficiently trained to meet these requirements.

The human resources department is responsible for ensuring that training records are maintained for each person.

The sales/marketing department is responsible for determining customer requirements and for ensuring customer satisfaction throughout the customer's experience with the product.

The engineering department is responsible for ensuring product development, design quality, research and development, manufacturing engineering, and product testing. The engineering department is also responsible for organizing design reviews and for ensuring that product designs are reliable.

The purchasing department is responsible for ensuring the quality of purchased materials, products, and services.

The manufacturing and production departments are responsible for fabrication, machining, assembly, and process inspection.

The accounting and finance departments are responsible for ensuring the quality of cost accounting, payroll, financial statement, and accounts payable information.

All organizational employees are responsible for quality. However, operational managers and supervisors have the additional responsibility for ensuring quality in terms of
- Identifying special quality process and product requirements,
- Identifying and recording quality problems,
- Providing resources, including training and equipment, to ensure that deficiencies do not recur,
- Initiating corrective action to prevent the recurrence or occurrence of a quality system deficiency, process instability, or product nonconformity,
- Initiating and recommending permanent solutions to correct deficiencies,
- Verifying implementation of the solution, and
- Monitoring the system to ensure that the deficiency does not recur.

The vice president of quality has the strict authority and responsibility for ensuring that ISO 9001 requirements are satisfied. Plant quality assurance managers and area managers also have the authority and responsibility for facilitating quality improvement.

Executive management formally reviews the organization's quality system at least once yearly to ensure continuing satisfaction of ISO 9001 requirements. ISO 9001 compliance review is conducted during the yearly state-of-the-organization or yearly shareholder meetings. Periodic reviews also may be conducted during monthly operation reviews or when there is sufficient cause. The chief executive officer, vice presidents, and their direct reports attend the meeting at headquarters. Operational heads, including department, unit, and plant managers report on the status of the quality initiatives within their purview. The agenda for the meeting may include
- ISO 9001 maintenance,
- Corrective action effectiveness,
- Customer satisfaction surveys,
- Recalls,
- Quality costs, and
- Scrap, rework, and warranty.

All ISO 9001 quality system requirements are evaluated during the yearly management review. As required, internal audits and corrective actions are conducted as required to maintain and to continue quality system improvement. The quality department is responsible for maintaining and distributing the records of all management quality reviews. If auditing or corrective actions are required, then the quality department is also responsible for conducting these.

## 4.2 QUALITY SYSTEM

*Purpose*

The purpose of this clause is to establish, document, and maintain a quality system to ensure that products and services conform to ISO 9001 requirements as well as satisfy external and internal customers.

*Policy*

The quality assurance department maintains the documented quality system. Four levels of quality documentation are

- *Quality manual.* First-level documentation consists of companywide quality policies.
- *Procedures manual.* Second-level documentation consists of quality assurance and control procedures.
- *Work instructions.* Third-level documentation is work-area, site, or process specific.
- *Forms and records.* Fourth-level documentation demonstrates or reports on ISO 9000 compliance.

Quality documentation is updated as required. The quality assurance department coordinates all revisions and distributes documentation to all authorized manual holders.

The quality and procedure manuals are controlled documents. Each owner is identified by name and manual number. Each manual has a list of other manual holders. Each manual holder is responsible for maintaining a current, complete, and accurate set of quality documents. Each manual holder is also responsible for reviewing, understanding, and implementing the changes in the revised or new pages. If the manual holder does not understand or agree with the change, then he or she may request assistance or clarification from the quality department.

The quality department is responsible for monitoring document distribution and compliance of quality documentation. The quality department is also responsible for maintaining the master copy of the quality and procedures manual. The quality department is responsible for defining, planning, and documenting how quality requirements are met.

Changes to the quality or procedures manuals may be submitted by any employee. The quality department is responsible for coordinating the changes.

## 4.3 CONTRACT REVIEW

*Purpose*

The purpose of this clause is to define, document, and ensure understanding of customer requirements, which may be specified in

- Purchase orders,
- Contracts,
- Specifications,
- Engineering drawings, and
- Verbal orders

*Policy*

The quality department is responsible for reviewing existing and ongoing contracts and purchase orders to ensure that the company has the capability to meet contractual requirements. The quality department is also responsible for reviewing modifications to existing contracts.

The quality department secures the assistance of the purchasing and engineering departments. Engineering personnel assist in evaluating changes in special or nonstandard products. Purchasing assists in securing information from suppliers. Marketing/sales assists in providing further customer information.

Contracts are thoroughly reviewed to verify that requirements are clearly defined, documented, and understood.

New contracts or modifications of existing contracts are accepted only when they have been subjected to a comprehensive review and signed off by the quality department. The quality department is also responsible for gathering the necessary information so it can be determined that the company has the ability to meet the requirements. The quality department is also responsible for gathering the necessary approvals or required information from other areas within the company.

All quality contract review information is retained in the quality assurance department.

## 4.4 DESIGN CONTROL

*Purpose*

The purpose of this clause is to describe a method for maintaining and documenting the integrity of designs to ensure that customers are satisfied and contractual requirements are met.

## *Policy*

All new designs or changes to existing designs are controlled and verified to ensure that product specifications are met. The engineering department approves all new designs or changes to existing designs.

The engineering and quality departments establish a plan that outlines the responsibility for each design and development activities to ensure compliance with specifications. The plan includes
- Identification of key product characteristics or changes to existing product,
- Customer requirements, including specifications,
- Key product or process attributes,
- Identification of how design changes affect existing products, and
- Identification of responsibilities.

The plan identifies key activities and assignments for ensuring that adequate and qualified resources are supplied for all project development.

The plan identifies organizational and technical interfaces for new product development, design changes, or process changes. The plan identifies interfaces for documenting, distributing, and reviewing design changes.

The plan identifies design input from all appropriate and reliable sources. Design input is identified, documented, and reviewed by department managers for completeness and accuracy. Incomplete or inaccurate requirements must be resolved to everyone's satisfaction before the design is approved.

Through the following design output considerations, the plan
- Ensures that output is documented and satisfies design input requirements,
- Identifies performance or acceptance criteria,
- Determines whether safety, health, or regulatory requirements are met, and
- Determines whether critical and major product attributes meet specifications.

✧ ✧ ✧

The plan identifies a procedure for verifying that design changes satisfy customer requirements. Design verification may be conducted through
- Scheduled design reviews,
- Testing and inspection,
- Calculation checks, and
- Comparative analysis.

The plan identifies a procedure for validating that the product conforms to user requirements. The quality department maintains records on all design reviews.

## 4.5 DOCUMENT AND DATA CONTROL

### *Purpose*

The purpose of this clause is to describe the methods, and responsibilities for controlling quality documentation and data which may be in written or electronic form.

### *Policy*

The quality manual incorporates ISO 9000 quality systems information that applies to the entire organization. Each department, plant, or work area may develop site-specific procedures and work instructions. All employees are encouraged to provide input for developing usable procedures and work instructions. All employees as well as new employees have been introduced to the quality manuals and their policies. All employees have been instructed on site-specific procedures and work instructions.

The site quality assurance (QA) coordinator maintains the original copy of departmental, plant, and site procedures and work instructions. The QA coordinator is responsible for revising, notifying, and transmitting controlled copies to authorized holders. The QA coordinator also communicates changes to the corporate department in order to ensure consistency in numbering, techniques, concepts, and nomenclature.

Work procedures and instructions must include the following for consistency:
- Original issue date,
- Current issue,

- Revision letter, if necessary,
- Procedure number, and
- Approvals.

The area or site QA coordinator is responsible for monitoring compliance of department, plant, and site procedures and work instructions. The coordinator is also responsible and has the authority to issue corrective actions.

Each authorized holder of a quality procedure or work instruction is required to review, understand, and implement the document's instructions.

The site QA coordinator assists the area management in developing documentation that indirectly relates to quality. The QA coordinator may assist the engineering manager or designee in complying with the ISO 9001 quality system requirements.

Each member of the organization is responsible for verifying that he or she has the latest revision of a quality documentation and data which may include
- Specifications or standards,
- Quality manual or policies,
- Quality procedures,
- Work instructions, and
- Engineering print or bills of material.

The site quality coordinator has a current master list of quality documentation. A description of the latest document revisions is located in each manual.

Changes to any plant, department, and site quality procedures and work instructions can be initiated by site personnel and must follow approved procedures. The area QA coordinator is responsible for communicating the formal revisions to the corporate quality department.

Each employee is responsible for promptly removing obsolete documents.

## 4.6 PURCHASING

*Purpose*

The purpose of this clause is to establish and maintain a quality system for ensuring that purchased materials and services satisfy internal and customer requirements.

*Policy*

Purchase orders or contracts clearly define the following product and service requirements:
- Technical and engineering,
- Commercial,
- Delivery,
- Service, and
- Quality.

Purchasing and quality departments are responsible for ensuring that quality requirements are complete, accurate, and understandable.

Suppliers are evaluated, monitored, and improved based on their ability to meet technical, commercial, delivery, service, and quality requirements. Supplier requirements are spelled out in the company's customer-supplier standard. Key prime suppliers are encouraged to become ISO 9000 registered. Otherwise suppliers are audited to the customer-supplier certification. Business is rewarded based on the results of the audit. Suppliers' subcontractors are expected to evaluate and select their suppliers based on ISO 9001 criteria.

The purchasing department is responsible for maintaining a list of approved or ISO 9000–certified suppliers. Supplier ratings are confidential. However, suppliers may request their evaluation reports. A supplier rating report is generated monthly for all key suppliers. The purchasing department is responsible for communicating this report to the supplier. The quality department is responsible for conducting the quality assessment and generating reports.

Purchase orders and contracts clearly describe the ordered products and services, including

- Number of products ordered,
- Precise identification,
- Drawing numbers,
- Bills of materials,
- Acceptance tests,
- Delivery and packaging instructions, and
- Other pertinent information.

Customers have the right to inspect, test, and otherwise ensure that requirements for products and services are met. Verifications of conformance may be done at the customer's facility or at this organization's.

## 4.7 Control of Customer-Supplied Product

### Purpose

The purpose of this clause is to establish consistent control of materials, products, and equipment supplied to this company by the customer.

### Policy

Customer-supplied product is any product, material, or equipment owned by the customer and supplied to this company to meet the customer's contractual requirements. This organization is responsible for the care and maintenance of the equipment until such time that the customer requests its return.

The customer-supplied products are secured, tagged, and used only for specified purposes.

If the customer's equipment does not conform to specifications, is damaged, is lost, or is out of calibration, the customer is immediately informed.

## 4.8 Product Identification and Traceability

### Purpose

The purpose of this clause is to establish guidelines and define a consistent method for ensuring product identification and traceability.

*Policy*

Key products purchased by this organization carry an identifying part number or other information that uniquely identifies the origin and date purchased of the product. The engineering, quality, and purchasing departments identify the products requiring unique identification numbers. These products are accompanied by documentation regarding their source.

A computer or bar-coded report is generated, is assigned to each incoming product shipment, and is entered into the computerized inventory tracking system.

The purchase order number and other documentation arriving with the supplied products indicate acceptance status. The acceptance status may be a stamp, tag, or label on the incoming supplied products. Or acceptance information may appear on the incoming supplier documentation.

A green stamp, tag, or label indicates that the supplied materials can go directly to production or inventory. If reduced receiving inspection is permitted, then this is indicated on the reduced inspection form.

All products manufactured by this organization are uniquely identified through routers, bills of material, work order numbers, tags, labels, or other identification that is used through incoming, in-process, and final production steps. Final products, as much as possible, are uniquely identified through a label or tag that has a serial number.

If the customer requires total traceability, then individual products are traced by these unique serial numbers.

## 4.9 Process Control

*Purpose*

The purpose of this clause is to establish guidelines and maintain a consistent method by which process control is established and maintained.

## Policy

Plant and operational managers are responsible for implementing and maintaining specific process control procedures and work instructions. Production planning, fabrication, assembly, testing, and other critical processes are controlled and documented on work orders, routers, and other production documentation. The flow of materials through production and assembly processes is detailed in work orders.

Documentation procedures and work instructions are approved by engineering, quality, and manufacturing staff assigned to the specific area. The ISO 9000 manufacturing representative or designate relays information to the corporate quality department concerning new quality documentation.

Area teams and process personnel are responsible for ensuring that suitable production and installation equipment is controlled and maintained.

All employees are responsible for the control, capability, and cleanliness of their work environment.

Process engineering, manufacturing, and quality personnel monitor and control process variables and product characteristics during production and installation. Process changes requiring new equipment or methods of operation must follow company procedures.

Workmanship criteria are defined for all critical processes to ensure internal and external customer satisfaction. The organization has identified special processes—such as welding and nondestructive testing—that are continuously monitored in accordance with manufacturing procedures. Appropriate documents are maintained in the quality department concerning the control and documentation of qualified processes, equipment, and personnel.

## 4.10 INSPECTION AND TESTING

### Purpose

The purpose of this clause is to establish guidelines for maintaining consistent inspection and testing.

*Policy*

The area quality representative is responsible for ensuring that receiving, in-process, and final inspection and testing are conducted according to quality procedures and work instructions.

Receiving inspection and testing follow quality procedures. Products are released for production through a waiver that is signed by the plant manager and the quality manager. Products released through a waiver are uniquely identifiable so that if product rework, replacement, or recall is required, then products can be retrieved.

In-process inspections and testing are conducted in accordance with specific procedures and instructions. Results are recorded in the appropriate forms. Inspectors refer to work orders, engineering drawings, inspection instructions, and other quality documentation for direction.

Nonconforming materials are properly segregated. Products do not proceed to the next step until all testing and inspections have been satisfactorily completed. Final inspection and testing are conducted according to specific procedures and instructions. Nonconforming materials are properly segregated and tagged upon discovery. Products do not proceed to the customer until all testing and inspection have been satisfactorily completed.

The process quality coordinator is responsible for the maintenance and control of inspection and test records. This individual keeps the corporate quality office notified of all procedure and work instruction changes.

Acceptance criteria are thoroughly defined for incoming, in-process, and final inspection and testing.

## 4.11 Control of Inspection, Measuring, and Test Equipment

*Purpose*

The purpose of this clause is to provide guidelines and to define a consistent method by which inspection, measuring, and test equipment is properly maintained and secured.

## *Policy*

The area quality coordinator is responsible for ensuring that this clause is implemented efficiently and effectively. The area quality coordinator is also responsible for ensuring that inspection, measuring, and test equipment are calibrated.

Calibration is conducted by external, certified laboratories. Calibration results are traceable to the National Institute of Standards and Technology (NIST). The company calibration procedures define acceptance criteria and calibration instructions. If an outside contractor conducts the calibration, then the contractor must supply assurance that its capabilities are traceable to NIST. The quality, engineering, and manufacturing departments determine the necessary precision and accuracy of inspection, measuring, and test equipment.

A master list of inspection, measuring, and equipment is maintained by the corporate quality organization. Area quality coordinators are responsible for ensuring the tagging and calibration of the inspection, measuring, and test equipment in their areas. The master list identifies the type of equipment, identification number, status, location, responsible party, and frequency of calibration. Inspection, measuring, and test equipment is labeled with a tag or sticker indicating the following:
- Identification number,
- Date of calibration,
- Location,
- Frequency of calibration, and
- Calibrator's name.

If a label or sticker won't adhere to the inspection, measuring, or test equipment, then other forms of traceable identification are used. The form of identification must be approved by the quality, engineering, and manufacturing departments.

Site or work area calibration is maintained by the area quality coordinator. This person reports on the status of all calibration within his or her jurisdiction to the corporate quality organization.

If inspecting, measuring, and test equipment is found to be out of calibration, a correction action request is issued to correct the problem. The quality department also conducts an audit to determine the validation of previous inspection and test results as well as the conformance of previously tested materials.

Environmental conditions are monitored and controlled during the use of identified test and measurement equipment. Test and measurement equipment is also handled, preserved, secured, and stored to maintain the required accuracy and precision.

No personal measurement equipment can be used without proper calibration and the approval of the area quality coordinator.

Inspection and testing software and hardware are controlled and monitored at intervals defined in procedures.

## 4.12 INSPECTION AND TEST STATUS

### *Purpose*

The purpose of this clause is to establish consistent guidelines for indicating inspection and test status.

### *Policy*

Area quality coordinators are responsible for ensuring the status of inspection and test equipment used in incoming, in-process, and final testing and inspection.

Incoming material inspectors ensure that supplied products are properly tested and segregated. Inspectors ensure that test results are readily available and physically attached to the shipment if possible.

In-process test and inspection personnel are responsible for indicating the status of in-process material on work orders, process sheets, routers, or other retrieval documentation. Final test and inspection personnel indicate on the appropriate document or record the test results.

Nonconforming materials or products are identified with a red hold tag and are segregated within the holding area. The area quality coordinator within two working days indicates the final disposition of the material.

## 4.13 Control of Nonconforming Product

### Purpose

The purpose of this clause is to provide guidelines and to establish a consistent method of controlling nonconforming products.

### Policy

Nonconforming incoming, in-process, and finished products are identified with a red label or reject tag. The nonconforming products are segregated to prevent use or installation. Nonconforming shipments are not entered into inventory or the inventory computerized list.

When a nonconformance is discovered, the area quality coordinator or representative is responsible for notifying the purchasing department. The purchasing department is responsible for notifying the product supplier about the nonconforming materials and for requesting disposition recommendations.

Repairs, returns, and rework are negotiated with the supplier. Products subject to rework or repairs are reinspected for conformance. The supplier is billed for any additional work.

The quality department is responsible for maintaining records of supplier nonconformances. Nonconforming shipments are tracked by the quality department.

The material review board (MRB) is responsible for reviewing the disposition of the nonconforming materials and issuing corrective action requests. Nonconforming products are reviewed by the purchasing, engineering, quality, and manufacturing departments. If necessary, the supplier may be audited by the quality department. If the supplier is not capable of delivering conforming shipments, the MRB is authorized to inform the purchasing department to secure a new supplier.

## 4.14 Corrective and Preventive Action

### *Purpose*

The purpose of this clause is to provide guidelines for establishing consistent methods for corrective and preventive action.

### *Policy*

Corrective action is initiated as a result of a quality system, process, or product deficiency. Any request for corrective action must be accompanied by a corrective action request (CAR) or a preventive action request (PAR) form.

Preventive action is initiated as a result of a customer complaint or to ensure corrective action efficiency. Any employee may initiate a corrective or preventive action request. CARs and PARs are sent to the area quality coordinator or to the corporate quality department. CARs and PARs are prioritized and then acted on. The initiator of the CAR or PAR is notified within one week about the status of the request. The quality department prioritizes CARs and PARs by risk and types of actions required. The initiating department or individual may select an individual to work with the quality organization to determine causes and to recommend solutions. The corporate quality department maintains copies of all CARs and PARs.

The quality department also may conduct follow-up audits of completed corrections to ensure that there are no recurring deficiencies. CAR and PAR changes in quality systems and processes are implemented and documented. The corporate quality department is notified about any changes.

Corrective and/or preventive action can be generated as a result of
- Customer complaints,
- High quality costs,
- Recurring deficiencies,
- Major product or process changes, and
- Operational inefficiencies or ineffectiveness.

## 4.15 Handling, Storage, Packaging, Preservation, and Delivery

*Purpose*

The purpose of this clause is to provide handling, storage, packaging preservation, and delivery guidelines.

*Policy*

Handling instructions and procedures for specific products are meant to prevent deterioration or damage. These documents are readily available throughout the organization. Personnel also have been instructed in how to handle these products.

Storage instruction and procedures for specific products are meant to prevent deterioration or damage. Outdoor storage facilities, stock rooms, inventory facilities, and holding areas are properly maintained to secure products and materials.

The conditions of materials, products, and equipment retained in storage areas are assessed regularly by inventory and quality personnel. Materials subject to degradation are evaluated periodically. Proper controls are established and followed to ensure the integrity of materials moved through production.

Packaging instructions and procedures for all products are consistently followed and are documented on product specification drawings. Packaging instructions are followed to ensure that products conform to requirements when delivered to the customer.

Delivery instructions and procedures ensure that materials and products are protected during shipment.

## 4.16 Control of Quality Records

*Purpose*

The purpose of this clause is to establish guidelines for controlling the identification, collection, indexing, filing, storage, and disposition of quality records.

*Policy*

Quality records support and document the quality practices and procedures of the organization. The quality department is responsible for maintaining a master list of current quality documents.

Records are complete, accurate, reliable, current, and usable. The records reflect the current state of quality from customer requirements, engineering, purchasing, manufacturing, calibration, inspection, and delivery of products.

Inspection and test records indicate
- Type of tests conducted,
- Sampling procedure,
- Results, and
- Type of deficiencies.

Quality records are maintained for at least five years, unless otherwise noted in a procedure. The quality department is responsible for maintaining a master list of quality procedures, documents, records, and forms. Depending on contractual requirements or special requests, the customer may be allowed access to the company's quality documentation.

## 4.17 INTERNAL QUALITY AUDITS

*Purpose*

The purpose of this clause is to provide guidelines for conducting quality audits.

*Policy*

Internal quality audit planning, implementation, and reporting are conducted per internal quality procedures.

The corporate quality department is responsible for
- An audit schedule,
- Audit frequency,
- Composition of the team,

- Managing the audit team,
- Planning and implementing the audit, and
- Reporting audit results.

Quality audits are conducted by personnel independent of the function being audited.

Each quality system of ISO 9001 is audited every six months. Audits are scheduled based on importance by the corporate quality department.

Nonconformances discovered as a result of the audit are reported through a corrective and preventive action request. The lead auditor reports the results to the responsible area manager at the conclusion of the audit. The area manager is responsible for responding to the corrective and preventive action recommendation within the time frame designated in the audit.

Corrective and preventive action requests are reported to the quality area coordinator and to the corporate quality department. If corrective and preventive action is not implemented within the designated time frame, then a second notice is sent to the area manager and to the business-unit manager.

A follow-up audit may be conducted on implementation of the corrective and preventive action to ensure that actions taken prevent recurrence of the problem.

## 4.18 TRAINING

### *Purpose*

The purpose of this clause is to establish a consistent method for training personnel in quality.

### *Policy*

The human resources department is responsible for
- Identifying company quality training requirements,
- Coordinating and delivering the training, and
- Ensuring that all employee records are current and complete.

❖ ❖ ❖

All company employees, as well as new employees, are trained in general company policies, including
- Customer quality requirements,
- Quality policies,
- Benefits,
- Labor rules,
- Work schedule, and
- Safety.

Department managers are responsible for reviewing employee training requirements and ensuring that area employees are properly trained. Training deficiencies are reported to the human resources department.

Human resources maintains training records of all company employees.

## 4.19 SERVICING

### *Purpose*

The purpose of this clause is to define a consistent method for controlling servicing.

### *Policy*

All products produced by this company have a limited warranty.

Quality policies, procedures, and work instructions in this manual apply to product servicing and installation.

Customer service personnel are responsible for ensuring and verifying that servicing meets requirements.

If a new situation or a special problem arises, customer service personnel are responsible for communicating with the engineering department to resolve the problem. Service personnel are also responsible for remaining current on the latest techniques and procedures for service, installation, and assembly.

## 4.20 Statistical Techniques

### Purpose

The purpose of this clause is to provide guidelines for using statistical techniques.

### Policy

Statistical techniques are used whenever possible in production and throughout the organization. Statistical process controls are used in production for critical process parameters. Cpk = 1.33 for critical process parameters. Statistical techniques are used in other areas wherever it's appropriate.

# SAMPLE QUALITY MANUAL 3*

### SECTION 1: MANAGEMENT RESPONSIBILITY

*Purpose*

The purpose of this section is to communicate and demonstrate Alpha's quality systems to all employees.

*Scope*

The policy applies to all employees and suppliers.

*Responsibility*

President of Alpha, Inc.

*Policy*

    1.1 The following quality policy statement was developed and established by the employees of Alpha and was approved by its board of directors. The policy is posted throughout our facilities, and all employees are expected to perform within its guidelines:

---

\* *Note:* This manual is aligned with ISO 9002. Two sections are not shown in this manual. Section 4, Design Control, is not part of ISO 9002. Section 19, Servicing, is not shown because the company, Alpha, is not required by the customer to service its products.

"Alpha's mission is to please its customers each and every time with the highest-quality, competitively priced products. Products are delivered right the first and every time by the most dependable and courteous employees in business. All of Alpha's employees are committed to these principles. If the customer at any time is dissatisfied with our products, we will gladly reimburse the customer or exchange products. Every Alpha employee is compensated based on his or her ability to consistently follow the above principles."

1.2 Alpha operates its quality systems to meet and to exceed ISO 9002 requirements. The quality system requirements outlined in this quality policies manual affect all employees.

1.3 Alpha's organizational chart describes the accountabilities, authorities, and interrelationships of Alpha personnel who manage, conduct, and verify activities concerning product quality. Alpha consists of functional units including quality, finance, purchasing, and manufacturing departments. These units have the following responsibilities:
- Quality is responsible for ISO 9002 maintenance, quality improvement, quality plans, training, testing, measuring equipment control, calibration, and all quality assurance activities.
- Marketing is responsible for sales, advertising, promotion, placement, and customer service.
- Manufacturing is responsible for producing, handling, preserving, and shipping products.
- Finance is responsible for money management, accounts payable, accounts receivable, accounting, costing, and human resources.

1.4 Alpha is an affirmative action employer. Job descriptions of all employees are maintained in the human resources department. These files are confidential and subject to the document control system outlined in Section 5 of this manual.

1.5 The vice president of quality is accountable for and has the authority to implement and maintain ISO 9002 requirements. The vice president of quality reports directly to the chief executive officer of Alpha.

1.6 Product requirements are specified in product
- Engineering prints,
- Bills of material,
- Standards and specifications,
- Work instructions,

- Quality inspection, testing, and verification instructions, and
- Sales orders.

1.7 All personnel are responsible for the quality of their activities. All personnel are trained in the following quality areas:
- Alpha's quality policies and procedures,
- Specific work instructions,
- Customer requirements,
- Engineering print interpretation, as required, and
- Basic quality principles and technologies.

1.8 The quality department conducts quality system audits every six months to ensure that all ISO 9002 requirements are being followed. Audit results are communicated to the chief executive officer and to the board of directors at the biyearly meeting. The vice president of quality
- Verifies the efficiency and effectiveness of Alpha's quality systems,
- Determines the cost of quality,
- Reports on corrective action and preventive requests issued since the last audit,
- Reports on the effectiveness of the corrective and preventive action requests since the last management review,
- Reports on the status of ISO 9002 maintenance, and
- Reports on customer returns.

1.9 Minutes of the formal management review are maintained by the quality department for five years.

## SECTION 2: QUALITY SYSTEM

### Purpose

The purpose of this section is to describe Alpha's quality system documentation and controls.

### Scope

The policy applies to Alpha's companywide quality systems.

## Responsibility

President of Alpha, Inc.
Quality vice president

## Policy

2.1 Alpha's quality initiative is outlined in the quality policies manual. This manual satisfies ISO 9002 requirements. Specific procedures and work instructions are covered in site-specific manuals. These quality documents cover all elements of Alpha's operation from understanding customer requirements to final delivery of products. These quality documents include the following support functions:
- Training,
- Document control,
- Quality auditing, and
- Test and measurement equipment calibration.

2.2 Quality procedures also identify authorities and accountabilities for Alpha's ISO 9002 quality systems.

2.3 The quality department maintains a complete, current, and accurate set of quality policies, procedures, and work instructions.

2.4. The quality department is responsible for drafting, approving, and distributing any revisions of a quality policy. Departments and business units can draft quality procedures and work instructions. Departments are responsible for sending the corporate quality department a final approved copy of a draft, original, or revised quality procedures and work instructions. The quality department is responsible for ensuring that departmental quality procedures and work instructions don't conflict with other quality documentation

2.5 The president of Alpha approves the quality policy manual and any revisions. Quality procedures, work instructions, test instructions, and other quality documentation are controlled and must comply with the provisions of the quality manual.

## SECTION 3: CONTRACT REVIEW

### *Purpose*

The purpose of this section is to ensure that each customer contract is reviewed and that customer requirements are defined.

### *Scope*

The policy applies to all of Alpha's customers and suppliers.

### *Responsibility*

Marketing vice president

### *Policy*

3.1 The marketing department is responsible for reviewing contracts and other incoming orders to ensure that Alpha is capable of satisfying customer requirements and orders.

3.2 Contracts and incoming orders are reviewed to verify that
- Customer requirements are defined,
- Process requirements are spelled out,
- Key product attributes are specified,
- Costs are spelled out,
- Delivery requirements are understood, and
- Technology requirements are understood.

3.3 Revisions to existing contracts are subject to the same review procedure as a new or original contract. Marketing, quality, and engineering jointly review the revisions to determine whether Alpha is capable of delivery.

3.4 The marketing department is responsible for maintaining records of contract and order review.

## SECTION 5: DOCUMENT AND DATA CONTROL

### Purpose

The purpose of this section is to ensure that the issue and revision of all quality documents and data affecting product and service quality are controlled.

### Scope

The policy applies to all ISO 9000 quality policies, procedures, work instructions, and other quality documents.

### Responsibility

Quality vice president

### Policy

5.1 The president of Alpha or a representative reviews and approves the quality policy manual each year for usability.

5.2 The quality policies manual is a controlled document. The designated quality policy manual holders are responsible for maintaining their quality manuals. They receive all new issues and revisions automatically. Quality manual holders are required to sign for receipt of the manuals and each policy revision. The quality department maintains the list of all quality manual holders.

5.3 When the quality manual is revised, the revision list in the manual is updated to show the current issue and forwarded along with the revision to all quality manual holders.

5.4 The quality department maintains the master copy of the quality manual. Copies of the manual may be issued to ISO 9000 auditors and to customers on approval of the quality department.

5.5 The quality department is responsible for issuing quality policies and procedures. Quality work instructions and other documents may be issued by plants and work sites.

5.6 A master copy of all revisions is maintained in the quality department.

5.7 All quality policies, procedures, and work instructions indicate the

- Issuance date,
- Revision date,
- Document identification number, and
- Authorized approval.

5.8 The quality department maintains a list of controlled and noncontrolled quality documents.

## SECTION 6: PURCHASING

### *Purpose*

The purpose of this section is to ensure that suppliers satisfy Alpha's requirements.

### *Scope*

The policy applies to all of Alpha's suppliers.

### *Responsibility*

Purchasing vice president

### *Policy*

6.1 Suppliers are responsible for understanding Alpha's requirements. Alpha provides all required information on request.

6.2 Suppliers are selected based on their ability to meet Alpha's quality, technology, delivery, and cost requirements. Past capability and performance are key elements for selecting suppliers.

6.3 Alpha's supplier requirements at a minimum detail the following:
- Product identification,
- Product and process requirements,
- Engineering drawings,
- Acceptance and inspection requirements, and
- Physical and chemical requirements.

6.4 Alpha reserves the right to audit suppliers to ensure compliance with contractual requirements. The supplier is notified of the audit at least two weeks prior to the audit.

## SECTION 7:
## CONTROL OF CUSTOMER-SUPPLIED PRODUCT

### Purpose

The purpose of this section is to describe a method of receiving and handling customer-supplied products.

### Scope

The policy applies to any product owned by the customer and provided to Alpha for satisfying a contract.

### Responsibility

Purchaser-supplied products are subject to the same processes and systems (such as receiving, inspection, product identification, storage, and handling procedures) as other Alpha products.

### Policy

7.1 Alpha notifies the customer if its products, gauges, or other equipment indicate any nonconformance. Nonconformance is identified and corrected through a work order or a corrective action request.

7.2 Departmental managers and area supervisors are responsible for storage, handling, and securing customer-supplied material in their work areas. The quality department or representative is responsible for monitoring the application of controls and procedures. At least every six months these procedures and implementation are audited.

7.3 Records of customer-supplied products are maintained by the quality department. If product or equipment users notice product nonconformance, then the quality department is immediately notified.

7.4 All customer-supplied products are subject to the same product identification and traceability requirements as Alpha's products.

## SECTION 8:
## PRODUCT IDENTIFICATION AND TRACEABILITY

### *Purpose*

The purpose of this section is to ensure that all materials are identified and traceable from receipt to shipping.

### *Scope*

The policy applies to all Alpha products.

### *Responsibility*

All Alpha departments

### *Policy*

8.1 Purchased products received at Alpha are assigned an identification number, which is entered into the computerized tracking system by the receiving dock personnel. Receiving personnel fill out the required paperwork and forward it to the quality department for confirmation and filing. After the identification number has been assigned, it becomes a permanent unique reference.

During in-process production, material is tracked using this reference number, thus providing total traceability.

All supplier information is recorded in the computer tracking system and becomes part of the master identification program.

8.2 The quality department or representative is responsible for auditing the effectiveness of the product identification and traceability system.

## SECTION 9: PROCESS CONTROL

### Purpose

The purpose of this section is to ensure that all processes affecting quality are carried out under controlled conditions. Processes are also in control and capable of meeting requirements.

### Scope

The policy applies to all critical Alpha processes.

### Responsibility

Quality vice president

### Policy

9.1 Written work instructions that define specific requirements are posted at critical work stations. The following are available at each critical work station:
- Work orders,
- Drawings,
- Bills of material,
- Special requirements,
- Work instructions, and
- Inspection instructions.

9.2 The quality and manufacturing departments jointly develop and authorize work and inspection instructions.

9.3 Workmanship criteria are based on customer requirements. Special work and inspection instructions may be developed depending on customers' requirements.

9.4 Workmanship and inspection instructions are developed by individual operations.

9.5 Departmental managers and site supervisors are responsible for establishing process control procedures and maintaining process control within their areas.

9.6 The quality department conducts quality audits to verify process control and capability of specified processes. The audits are conducted at least every six months.

## SECTION 10: INSPECTION AND TESTING

### *Purpose*

The purpose of this section is to ensure that quality control procedures are implemented so that products meet customers' requirements.

### *Scope*

The policy applies to all inspection areas, including incoming, in-process, and final inspections.

### *Responsibility*

Quality assurance
Manufacturing management or representatives

### *Policy*

10.1 Receiving inspection and testing are conducted per quality procedures and inspection instructions. No materials are released to production until the required receiving, in-process, or final inspections are completed.

10.2 Independent verifications of supplier certifications are conducted by ABC Laboratories.

10.3 In-process inspection and testing are completed per quality procedures.

10.4 Critical parts are inspected and tested so that they meet Alpha's requirements. Verification and validation that parts meet specified requirements are completed per Alpha inspection procedures. The inspector signs the shipping tags to indicate approval to move parts to the next operation. Inspection procedures control and document all receiving, in-process, and final inspection operations. This form serves as evidence that the product has passed the required inspections. The manufacturing department is responsible for maintaining the files.

10.5 Product inspection and testing are conducted as required to verify that documentation quality plans, instructions, and standards are adequate to ensure that product specifications meet Alpha procedures. One hundred percent inspection and testing on critical parts are conducted at least once a month.

10.6 Product inspection and testing are conducted by the plant quality manager or representative. Products are selected at random and are representative of production lots. All product characteristics as specified on engineering prints are tested and/or inspected. Unusual patterns or measurement outside specifications are brought to the attention of the manufacturing manager and to the plant manager. Operations are suspended until the symptom and the root cause can be analyzed and eliminated.

10.7 During product inspection and testing, if a part is out of tolerance, then, depending on a joint evaluation by the manufacturing and quality managers, all parts may be 100 percent inspected. The quality manager or representative issues a corrective action request.

10.8 Machine capability studies are conducted on critical process characteristics weekly by manufacturing personnel according to procedures.

10.9 Thirty minimum samples are taken for the process capability study. Capability measurement and ranges are posted at each machine.

## SECTION 11: CONTROL OF INSPECTION, MEASURING, AND TEST EQUIPMENT

### Purpose

The purpose of this section is to ensure that control is maintained over measuring and test equipment.

### Scope

The policy applies to all measuring and test equipment used to verify the quality of products and processes.

## *Responsibility*

Quality manager or representative

## *Policy*

11.1 Inspection, measuring, and test equipment is maintained and controlled by the quality department. The quality department is also responsible for ensuring that all equipment is calibrated and properly tagged.

11.2 Calibration is conducted according to the measurement and test equipment procedure. All calibration is traceable to the National Institute of Standards and Technology (NIST).

11.3 The master list of inspection, measurement, and test equipment is maintained in the quality assurance department. The master list outlines the equipment, type, identification number, location, and frequency of calibration.

11.4 Test and measurement equipment tolerances are calibrated at least in a ten-to-one ratio of measurements taken during production.

11.5 Alpha employees are responsible for verifying that inspection, measurement, and test equipment is calibrated properly. All calibrated equipment is identified according to its calibration status.

11.6 If an Alpha employee identifies a piece of equipment that is out of calibration, then the person should immediately notify the quality department about the situation.

11.7 Out-of-calibration measurement and test equipment is investigated by the quality department to determine the validity of previous inspection and test results. Deficient-calibration equipment is immediately calibrated, and the systems that allowed for the deficiency are corrected.

11.8 The quality department evaluates calibration records for any indication that measurement and test equipment is not suitable for its purpose. In this situation, the quality representative makes recommendations for selecting the proper equipment. The quality representative uses the manufacturer's specifications for measurement equipment and its use to determine suitability.

11.9 The quality department ensures that handling, preservation, and storage of inspection, measurement, and test equipment are suitable for maintaining the required accuracy. The quality department checks all equipment at least every six months.

11.10 Out-of-calibration measurement and test equipment is repaired, destroyed, or replaced. Authorized dealers or sources repair equipment. Alpha employees do not make adjustments to measurement and test equipment.

11.11 All inspection, measurement, and test equipment used in Alpha is solely owned and dedicated to maintaining quality. Alpha employees use privately owned measurement equipment. All Alpha measurement equipment is used to ensure that measurement uncertainty and repeatability are recognized and within acceptable limits.

11.12 The following equipment may also be evaluated:
- Jigs,
- Fixtures,
- Templates, and
- Patterns.

11.13 Quality and manufacturing personnel ensure that testing and measurement are conducted under controlled conditions. Temperature, humidity, particulate, and other environmental conditions are checked to ensure that they don't affect production and measurement quality. As much as possible, calibration environmental conditions are suitable to test and measurement.

## SECTION 12: INSPECTION AND TEST STATUS

### Purpose

The purpose of this section is to ensure that all inspection and test results and status are identified throughout the manufacturing process.

### Scope

The policy applies to all Alpha manufacturing products.

### Responsibility

Manufacturing personnel

## Policy

12.1 Inspection and test results and status are identified throughout manufacturing. Only products passing inspections are processed.

12.2 Each lot, batch, or group of products is identified by a label, tag, or other identification. Each process step issues a numbered identification tag or label for the product manufactured. The operator or inspector indicates on the tag the inspection or testing performed at that station.

12.3 The operator is responsible for ensuring that the test status of the material received from an upstream process step has satisfied required inspection and testing. Nonconforming materials are segregated immediately and held in the reject, scrap, and rework area.

# SECTION 13:
# CONTROL OF NONCONFORMING PRODUCT

## Purpose

The purpose of this section is to ensure that nonconforming materials are isolated and controlled.

## Scope

The policy applies to nonconforming materials identified by the customer or Alpha personnel.

## Responsibility

Production, quality, and operating personnel.

## Policy

13.1 Incoming, in-process, and finished products that don't conform to specified requirements are tagged or labeled with a unique identification. The nonconforming products are segregated and held in the reject, scrap, and rework area.

13.2 Segregated nonconforming materials can't be used unless the quality and manufacturing departments approve the release to manufacturing.

13.3 Disposition of nonconforming materials must be done within one business day.

13.4 Incoming nonconforming materials and products are returned to the supplier within three working days.

13.5 Repaired or reworked products are reclassified as conforming after approval testing by quality personnel.

13.6 Nonconforming materials are reviewed and analyzed by quality personnel. If necessary, quality department personnel initiate a corrective action request.

## SECTION 14: CORRECTIVE AND PREVENTIVE ACTION

### Purpose

The purpose of this section is to ensure that corrective and preventive action is implemented by the responsible department and to eliminate the recurrence of the nonconformance.

### Scope

The policy applies to out-of-control processes and nonconforming materials that are identified throughout Alpha.

### Responsibility

Quality assurance managers or representatives

### Policy

14.1 Nonconforming materials are identified and disposed of according to policies outlined in this manual. The corrective action request should eliminate the symptom, root cause, chronic, or systemic problem. The quality department maintains corrective action requests and preventive action requests.

14.2 Any Alpha employee may request an audit, initiate a corrective action request or initiate a preventive action request.

14.3 CARs result from an audit and then are forwarded to the area where correction is required. The departmental manager or representative on implementing the CAR is required to return the form to the quality department.

14.4 The department with the problem must implement changes in procedures, processes, and documents where applicable. Each departmental manager has thirty days to respond to the CAR. Depending on the severity of the problem, the manager may request an extension to eliminate the root cause.

14.5 Every six months the quality department monitors work operations, quality documentation, customer complaints, cost of quality, and other quality indicators to eliminate the potential cause of quality deficiencies. As required, operating departments or the quality department can initiate a preventive action request.

14.6 Suppliers are also expected to implement quality audits, initiate corrective action requests, and ensure that quality problems don't recur.

## SECTION 15:
## HANDLING, STORAGE, PACKAGING, PRESERVATION, AND DELIVERY

### Purpose

The purpose of this section is to ensure the safe, efficient, effective handling of materials, products, and equipment in order to prevent deficiencies.

### Scope

The policy applies to all products.

### Responsibility

All operating departments

*Policy*

15.1 All operating departments follow Alpha handling, storage, and delivery policies and procedures. Each department handling materials can develop procedures controlling quality handling, storage, and delivery. All products supplied, processed, and delivered to Alpha customers are identified, preserved, and segregated from receipt to delivery. Identification is through physical tagging to computerized identification.

15.1 All Alpha departments handle materials, products, and equipment in order to prevent damage or deterioration. Departmental procedures establish appropriate methods for the authorization of receipt and distribution of materials.

15.3 All Alpha departments suitably store materials, products, and equipment in order to prevent damage or deterioration. Storage bays and in-process storage areas provide adequate security and are maintained to prevent damage or deterioration. Alpha products are processed in a first-in and first-out basis. Incoming, in-process, and final processed products are inspected randomly.

15.4 All Alpha departments package materials, products, and equipment in order to prevent damage or deterioration. Packaging instructions and tag identification are specified by work orders, specifications, or customer requests.

## Section 16: Control of Quality Records

*Purpose*

The purpose of this section is to ensure that quality records are available on all products manufactured.

*Scope*

The policy applies to all quality documentation and records.

*Responsibility*

Quality department

## Policy

16.1 Quality records are maintained by the quality department. The quality records files demonstrate the maintenance and prevention initiatives at Alpha.

16.2 Quality records are identified, collected, indexed, filed, and disposed of according to Alpha policies and procedures.

16.3 Department managers are responsible for determining the usability, accuracy, currentness, and completeness of quality documentation in their work areas.

16.4 The quality department or representative is responsible for reviewing the quality documents, quality systems, and quality processes.

16.5 The following quality documentation is maintained in the quality department:
- Quality policies,
- Quality procedures,
- Quality instructions,
- Quality audits,
- Corrective action requests, and
- Management reviews.

# SECTION 17: INTERNAL QUALITY AUDITS

## Purpose

The purpose of this section is to ensure that all quality systems are in place and working properly, that quality documentation reflects ISO 9000 requirements, and that quality process improvements are implemented.

## Scope

The policy applies to all quality procedures and personnel.

## Responsibility

Quality department

*Policy*

17.1 Internal quality audits are conducted every six months to determine ISO 9002 compliance. Internal audits are also conducted if there are changes to quality systems, processes, and procedures. The quality department is responsible for the audit schedule, audit frequency, and composition of the audit team.

17.2 Audits are scheduled based on the importance of the situation. The quality department has the responsibility and authority to prioritize audit requests. All quality systems are audited every six months.

17.3 Operations and departments to be audited are notified as to the schedule of the audit and implementation.

17.4 The quality auditor initiates a corrective action request (CAR) if deficiencies are discovered. CARs are sent to the responsible department manager. The auditor and the auditee discuss and negotiate the due date for the corrective action. Reports are issued to the responsible manager and copied to the following departments:
- Engineering,
- Manufacturing,
- Quality, and
- Purchasing.

17.5 The quality manager or representative is responsible for ensuring that quality audits are conducted properly, corrective actions are implemented, and quality actions are effective. The responsible department has thirty days to implement the changes recommended in the CAR.

17.6 Quality audit and CAR records are kept in the quality department.

## SECTION 18: TRAINING

*Purpose*

The purpose of this section is to ensure that all employees understand the quality requirements of their jobs.

*Scope*

The policy applies to all employees.

*Responsibility*

All employees

*Policy*

18.1 The training department is responsible for developing and maintaining training information about all Alpha training. The training department develops training requirements for all Alpha personnel.

18.2 The training department trains all new Alpha personnel on the key elements of this quality policies manual.

18.3 All existing and new employees are required to complete Alpha's training program. The training department also evaluates the training needs of each position and compares these needs with the individual performing the work. If additional training is required of existing or new employees, the trainer discusses training requirements with area supervision and the individual and then recommends training support.

18.4 The training department maintains records of each employee's training.

## SECTION 20: STATISTICAL TECHNIQUES

*Purpose*

The purpose of this section is to ensure that statistical techniques are used where appropriate.

*Scope*

The policy applies to all appropriate Alpha processes.

*Responsibility*

Plant manager
Manufacturing vice president

## Policy

20.1 All Alpha employees are taught statistical techniques, including statistical process control. The quality or training department conducts the training.

20.2 The manufacturing department is responsible for applying statistical techniques to production operations. Key product attributes are controlled. Manufacturing is responsible for establishing the control and capability of critical process parameters.

# SAMPLE QUALITY MANUAL 4

## 1.0 MANAGEMENT RESPONSIBILITY

Manufacturing Incorporated (MI) management and the organization have developed the following companywide quality policy:

"Manufacturing, Inc. believes that total customer satisfaction achieved through total quality is the prime requirement for the company. The company satisfies customers through understanding requirements and expectations. These requirements are met each time, every time, and on time."

The company excels at product and service quality, delivery, service, cost, and technology to satisfy its customers.

MI's quality systems satisfy ISO 9001 requirements.

MI's chief executive is responsible for the overall quality initiative. The details of the quality policy manual are delivered to the quality vice president. This person is the management representative for the organization and has the full authority to identify quality problems, to initiate correction actions to eliminate any root causes and symptomatic problems, and to initiate preventive actions to search for improvement opportunities.

MI management is responsible for ensuring that operations comply with the requirements of the quality manual and the procedures manual. The quality policy manual defines the quality requirements of MI. All MI employees are responsible for quality systems, processes, and products.

The organizational chart of the company defines the interrelationships between company employees and indicates quality authorities and responsibilities:
- The chief executive officer and the quality vice president are responsible for the overall quality program.
- Area quality coordinators have the authority and responsibility for initiating positive action to prevent the occurrence or recurrence of process instabilities and product nonconformances.
- All MI employees have the authority and responsibility for identifying quality problems and for initiating a corrective action requests for ineffective or inefficient operations.
- The quality department is responsible for conducting the investigation of corrective action requests.

MI management formally reviews the organization's quality systems to ensure that customer requirements are continually being met.

## 2.0 QUALITY SYSTEM

MI has defined, developed, implemented, and maintained quality systems that meet ISO 9001 requirements. The quality system is defined and documented in the quality policies manual, quality procedures manual, and quality work instructions.

MI's quality systems are periodically evaluated to ensure continued effectiveness in controlling MI's processes and products. If changes occur in the company's quality systems, policies, procedures, and instructions are updated as required.

## 3.0 CONTRACT REVIEW

MI ensures upon receiving a customer order that it understands the customer's quality requirements and is capable of meeting these requirements.

Customers' requirements are preferably defined in written form.

## 4.0 Design Control

MI procedures and work instructions ensure that the design and development of products are planned, controlled, and verified so that customer requirements are satisfied. An important element is to ensure that health and safety regulatory requirements are satisfied.

## 5.0 Document and Data Control

All MI documents, specifications, standards, data and other quality documents are controlled according to quality procedures. All revisions to existing quality documents are sent to authorized holders of quality documentation to ensure that MI employees have the most current quality documentation. Outdated documents are destroyed.

## 6.0 Purchasing

MI selects its suppliers based on quality and cost criteria. MI monitors and controls its suppliers through monthly reviews of critical suppliers. Results are shared with suppliers.

Suppliers must have the capability to provide products and services that satisfy MI's requirements and that arrive on time. Corrective actions are expected to be prompt.

MI reserves the right to refuse products that don't meet all requirements.

## 7.0 Control of Customer-Supplied Product

MI does not use customers' products or equipment in manufacturing its own products.

## 8.0 Product Identification and Traceability

MI uses labels and tags to ensure product identification throughout the organization. Identified employees are responsible for the correct identification of parts, subassemblies, assemblies, and final products to ensure total traceability.

❊ ❊ ❊

If a customer contract specifies proof of traceability, the quality department is responsible for contacting the customer and ensuring that requirements are satisfied.

## 9.0 PROCESS CONTROL

MI identifies key product attributes and controls key process variables relating to these product attributes. The following are essential elements of process control:
- Operators and teams are responsible for process control and product quality,
- Employees are trained in quality,
- Work instructions are process and product specific,
- Measurement and test equipment are calibrated,
- Equipment and processes are approved and monitored, and
- Workmanship standards are defined for all quality activities.

Formal documented procedures are developed and followed so that processes and measurement equipment are capable.

## 10.0 INSPECTION AND TESTING

Incoming inspection confirms that the materials delivered comply with MI specifications.

In-process inspection ensures that production and assembly products meet MI requirements. Operators are responsible for monitoring the quality of products being used and for controlling their processes. Operators are responsible for inspecting products, for segregating nonconforming products, and for controlling their processes.

Final inspection ensures that all products are tested and meet MI product requirements.

Records of all inspection and testing are maintained by the quality department.

## 11.0 Control of Inspection, Measuring, and Test Equipment

MI affirms the importance of accurate and precise inspection, measuring, and test equipment to maintain product quality. A comprehensive calibration system covers all MI's critical inspection equipment used to validate product conformance to requirements. All inspection, measurement, and test equipment is traceable to the National Institute of Standards and Technology (NIST).

## 12.0 Inspection and Test Status

MI manufacturing personnel are responsible for identifying the inspection and test status of incoming, in-process, and final processed products. All nonconforming and unsuitable products are identified and segregated.

## 13.0 Control of Nonconforming Product

MI personnel during incoming, in-process, and final inspection identify nonconforming products, determine the rework or scrap status, and determine disposition.

## 14.0 Corrective and Preventive Action

MI has a corrective and preventive action quality system to identify problems and to eliminate their root causes. Any MI employee can initiate a corrective action request. The material review board (MRB) conducts monthly formal reviews of all scrap, waivers, customer complaints, outstanding CARs, and cost of quality. If deficiencies recur, the MRB has the authority to request an internal audit.

## 15.0 Handling, Storage, Packing, Preservation, and Delivery

MI has proper handling equipment and trained personnel to ensure the swift and precise movement of materials and products. Disposition areas are defined for the storage of special products.

Packaging instructions and specifications are developed for all products to ensure customer satisfaction on delivery.

## 16.0 QUALITY RECORDS

MI has records of all activities related to the control of process and product quality. These records are available to customers on request. Computerized and written records include product test and inspection results, process charts, quality reports, and other records. These records are retained for five years.

## 17.0 INTERNAL QUALITY AUDITS

MI ensures the effectiveness of internal quality control systems by performing internal audits of 100 percent of its internal quality systems at least every six months. Internal quality auditors conduct these audits according to generally accepted quality auditing principles. These audits result in corrective action requests that are aimed at eliminating root-cause deficiencies and also improving the quality systems.

## 18.0 TRAINING

MI trains all its employees in quality. The company considers its employees crucial in the control of its systems, processes, and products.

All employees are also trained in job-specific skills. Yearly, the human resources department evaluates internal job requirements and determines individual training needs. Training records are maintained in the human resources department.

## 19.0 SERVICING

MI employees service products through a documented service control and delivery procedure. Service employees are trained in the latest technical requirements in order to service its field machines.

## 20.0 STATISTICAL TECHNIQUES

MI has identified specific production processes to determine where statistical techniques are appropriate.

# SAMPLE QUALITY PROCEDURES

# ISO 9001 CLAUSE 4.1: MANAGEMENT RESPONSIBILITY

## QUALITY DEPARTMENT ORGANIZATION

### Purpose

The purpose of this procedure is to outline the quality department's functional responsibilities.

### Scope

This procedure applies to all quality department personnel.

### Procedure

The major quality functional areas are quality management, quality engineering, quality assurance, and quality control. All these functions report to the quality vice president.

QUALITY MANAGEMENT

The quality vice president reports directly to the president of the company. This person is responsible for the overall management and direction of the quality activities, including ensuring that

- External and internal customers are satisfied,
- Products and services satisfy contract requirements, and
- Regulatory requirements are satisfied.

Quality management is also responsible for complying with ISO 9000 requirements, including

- Defining and documenting quality responsibilities, objectives, policies,
- Defining organizational quality responsibilities and authorities,
- Authorizing sufficient resources to perform and to verify quality activities,
- Serving as the organization's management quality representative for complying with ISO 9000 requirements, and
- Reviewing periodically the quality systems to ensure effectiveness and suitability for satisfying ISO 9000 requirements.

QUALITY ENGINEERING

Quality engineering has the following responsibilities:

- Developing, implementing, and evaluating tests and processes for ensuring that quality specifications and customer requirements are satisfied,

- Determining whether customer requirements can be satisfied with company resources and capabilities (if customer requirements are beyond the organization's capabilities, quality engineering assesses and seeks authorization of capital monies or external resources to satisfy requirements),
- Participating in preparing bids and other contract documents involving quality,
- Providing engineering assistance with capability studies, specification development, and other technical matters,
- Reviewing engineering drawings to identify key product attributes, capability studies, and conformance to customer requirements, and
- Assisting suppliers in conforming to contract requirements.

QUALITY ASSURANCE

Quality assurance has the following responsibilities:
- Reviewing customer requirements, contracts, and other information to determine whether the organization has the capabilities to satisfy them,
- Developing and writing policies, procedures, and work instructions that comply with ISO 9000 requirements,
- Auditing internal operations to ensure compliance with policies and procedures,
- Developing quality plans for all existing and new projects and products to ensure that quality requirements are defined and complied with,
- Preparing weekly, monthly, and quarterly quality reports, and
- Representing the department in quality-related activities.

QUALITY CONTROL

Quality control has the following responsibilities:
- Identifying, inspecting, and testing materials from outside suppliers to ensure conformance with requirements, evaluating supplier history, and documenting results of the inspection,
- Identifying, inspecting, and testing materials and products while in-process,
- Identifying, inspecting, and testing completed products, including first-article inspection, final test, and system test,
- Evaluating special tools, dies, and test equipment for conducting inspections and tests,
- Performing or ensuring that calibrations are performed properly, and
- Ensuring that calibration is properly documented.

# ISO 9001 CLAUSE 4.2: QUALITY SYSTEM

## Quality Planning

### *Purpose*

The purpose of this procedure is to provide guidelines for planning and conducting a quality evaluation of existing and new contracts.

### *Scope*

This procedure applies to all quality department personnel involved in program development, product evaluation, contract negotiation, or supplier evaluation.

### *Procedure*

The quality department consults with the purchasing and engineering departments during the contract bidding, evaluation, or assessment phase. The quality department evaluates customer requirements to determine whether the organization can satisfy them in-house. The results of the evaluation are forwarded to purchasing, engineering, and sales. Additional requirements for satisfying the contract are documented and reported, including
- Personnel,
- Test and measurement equipment,
- Outside consultants or suppliers, and
- Machining and other production equipment.

On acceptance of the contract, the quality department reviews appropriate customer documents and develops a plan for ensuring compliance with its quality requirements. The plan addresses the following:
- Product attributes,
- Process control and capability,
- Quality costs,
- Certifications,
- Inspection and sampling methods,
- Inspection, test, and measurement equipment,
- Inspection points,
- Supplier evaluation,

- Quality auditing,
- Tasks for ensuring quality, and
- First-article inspection.

The quality control supervisor or designated representative reviews the inspection plan and prepares specific work instructions for ensuring that all customer and internal quality requirements are satisfied. Instructions also address criteria for acceptable or unacceptable workmanship.

All quality plans are reviewed by the appropriate departments, including engineering, purchasing, manufacturing, and sales. Quality plans are available at each of the main functional departments, plants, and other required sites.

The quality department ensures that all quality plan requirements are being satisfied through periodic audits.

## QUALITY SYSTEMS PLANNING

### *Purpose*

This procedure details a plan for designing, manufacturing, and delivering a product.

### *Scope*

This procedure applies to all quality, engineering, purchasing, and logistical departments responsible for providing input about new and existing contracts.

### *Procedure*

The quality department is responsible for obtaining and distilling customer quality requirements. The quality department is also responsible for procuring quality resources information from
- Marketing and sales,
- Manufacturing,
- Engineering,
- Purchasing, and
- Logistics.

The marketing and sales department provides information about service requirements, after-sales service, field maintenance, and other quality-related issues. The manufacturing, planning, and control departments examine and detail specific manufacturing processes to comply with contract requirements. This examination identifies specific production operations, the sequence of operations, test and measurement equipment, test and measurement inspection points, special fixtures and gauges, special methods of operation, and other production-related information. The engineering department provides preliminary drawings, specifications, test requirements, supplied materials lists, and other technical related information. The purchasing department provides a preliminary suppliers' list. Logistics provides information about handling, packaging, storage, and delivery.

The quality department collates the above information and develops a quality plan identifying the following:
- Plan number,
- Program, project, and customer identification,
- Product, assembly, subassembly, and part number,
- Team and individual team members,
- Product quality requirements,
- Product attributes to be verified,
- Method of testing product attributes,
- Location of where testing occurs,
- Methods of testing, and
- Inspection, test, and measurement equipment identification.

The quality department gathers the above logistical information and develops a plan to identify proper storage, handling, preservation, packaging, shipping instructions to prevent product damage, degradation, and deterioration. The quality department collates the above purchasing information to identify possible suppliers. In addition, the quality department determines supplier selection, assessment, and improvement methods.

The quality department evaluates preliminary engineering designs, reliability tests, calculations, and other technical information. Prior to release, the quality plan is evaluated by appropriate personnel in marketing/sales, engineering, manufacturing, purchasing, and logistics.

On acceptance of the contract, the quality plan is released for detailed engineering drawings, production plans, supplier selection, and product packaging.

## ISO 9001 CLAUSE 4.3: CONTRACT REVIEW

### NEW CONTRACT REQUIREMENTS

*Purpose*

This procedure details the process for understanding and satisfying new contract requirements.

*Scope*

This procedures applies to new and existing customer contracts.

*Procedure*

The marketing and sales department is responsible for obtaining copies of new contracts, engineering prints, delivery, quality, service, and cost information. Marketing and sales is also responsible for disseminating the information to the appropriate departments. This information is gathered during the supplier assessment and bid steps of the contract. On acceptance of the contract, the marketing and sales department also continues to gather information about contract changes.

The quality department is responsible for evaluating the quality requirements of the new contract. The quality department undertakes a complete analysis of the new contract and informs the marketing and sales, engineering, manufacturing, service, and purchasing departments about the new or pending contract quality requirements.

The quality department or designated team identifies the following contract requirements:
- Customer name,
- Contract number,
- Type of contract,
- Regulatory authorities,
- Regulatory requirements,

- Product or service description,
- Start date of contract,
- End date of contract,
- Number of units ordered,
- Schedule of delivery,
- Quality requirements of product or service,
- Unusual quality specifications or requirements,
- Special engineering or technical requirements,
- Special measurement or inspection equipment, and
- Special methods or operational procedures.

The quality department or designated team identifies the following capabilities:
- Customer name,
- Contract name,
- Type of contract,
- Product description,
- Regulatory requirements, and
- List of contract requirements:
  - Regulatory,
  - Technical,
  - Quality,
  - Cost,
  - Delivery, packaging, and handling,
  - Service,
  - Identification and location of existing resources to satisfy the above requirements,
  - Identification of new resources to satisfy the above requirements,
  - Approximation of costs to secure new resources to satisfy above requirements,
  - Designation of the team responsible for securing new resources, and
  - Project completion date.

The quality department is responsible for monitoring and reporting about the project completion of assignments, resources allocation, and dates to the management committee.

## ISO 9001 CLAUSE 4.4: DESIGN CONTROL

### ENGINEERING DRAWING REVIEW

*Purpose*

The purpose of this procedure is to define the requirements for a preliminary evaluation of engineering drawings or design changes so that customer requirements are addressed and complied with.

*Scope*

This procedure applies to the quality and engineering departments.

*Procedure*

All initial engineering drawings, changes, or revisions are reviewed and approved by quality department representatives. The quality department reviews and signs any designs prior to release to production, suppliers, and other interested parties.

The quality department is responsible for reviewing the drawings to ensure that
- Quality requirements are spelled out,
- Product quality attributes are identified,
- Process requirements are spelled out,
- Proper materials are called out,
- Process capability and control requirements are spelled out,
- Special process specifications are identified,
- Government, customer, or regulatory requirements are identified,
- Bills of materials are complete, and
- Special instructions are complete, current, and understandable.

After review, if the drawings or revisions are acceptable, the quality engineering representative signs and approves the drawings and returns them to engineering within five working days. If the quality engineering reviewer has questions or discovers discrepancies in the documents, the quality engineering reviewer coordinates these with the design engineering supervisor. If an engineering change is required, the quality engineering reviewer initiates the change order.

## Design Review, Documentation Review, and Control

### Purpose

This procedure describes the review and analysis of engineering drawings, specifications, and other technical documentation for adequacy, completeness, currentness, and understandability. In-house and supplier operations are monitored to ensure that modifications to technical documentation are incorporated efficiently and effectively.

### Scope

This procedure applies to the quality and engineering departments for
- Engineering drawings,
- Standards,
- Specifications,
- Procedures,
- Bills of materials,
- Work instructions,
- Purchase orders,
- Engineering change orders,
- Process instructions, and
- Production engineering instructions.

### Procedure

The quality department is responsible for reviewing engineering designs and documentation. The quality department forms a team of interested individuals to conduct the review. Representatives from the manufacturing, engineering, purchasing, marketing, and other departments may be on the team. Key suppliers also may be included in the design review team.

Criteria to be considered in the review are
- Adequacy,
- Accuracy,
- Completeness,
- Currentness,
- Understandability, and
- Precision.

Audits and assessments are conducted periodically and throughout the design process to ensure that the above criteria are satisfied. The audits are planned and organized by the quality department. Discrepancies result in a corrective action request (CAR).

After the design has been approved, then periodic and random audits are conducted to ensure that only current documents are distributed and used. Obsolete materials are removed.

The quality department is responsible for reviewing and analyzing all existing records for effectiveness and improvement. If improvements are noted, then these are forwarded to the engineering and other departments for implementation.

The material review board and the change control board review and approve all modifications of materials and designs. The quality department serves as staff to the above two boards. The boards are authorized to approve reviews and audits of material and design changes.

The quality department is responsible for monitoring the incorporation of design, manufacturing, supplier changes as required by the corrective action request.

## DESIGN REVIEW PROCESS

### *Purpose*

This procedure describes the quality design review process.

### *Scope*

This procedure applies to new designs and modifications of existing designs.

### *Procedure*

All new and modified designs are reviewed. Design review occurs when a product is being developed, when a product or process change occurs, or when a new product is being considered. A team from the affected departments is formed to review drawings. The team is comprised of representatives from the engineering, quality, manufacturing, and marketing departments, from suppliers, and from other affected parties.

Each new or pending contract is reviewed for understandability and compliance. Design input, design output, and final use are also evaluated. Options and actions required are also discussed and determined by the team.

The team also addresses the following criteria for final use:
- Who are probable and possible customers?
- What requirements must be considered in this contract:
  Regulatory,
  International,
  National, or
  Industry?
- What is the product's intended quality level?
- What are the product's life expectancy, reliability, and maintainability requirements?
- What are the environmental considerations for the design?
- What are the safety and health considerations for the design?
- Are there any other important considerations?

The team considers the following storage and handling criteria:
- What are the environmental considerations for the design?
- Is moisture, humidity, thermal, or other protection required?
- What are the shelf-life and special aging requirements?
- Are there special packaging and shipping requirements?

The team considers the following production criteria:
- Are production procedures and work instructions written?
- Does the design require special production processes, fixtures, or gauges?
- Are design tolerances realistic in terms of maintaining process control, capability, and improvement?
- Does new equipment need to be purchased?

The team considers the following measurement and test criteria:
- Are qualification or first-item tests required?
- Have measurement, test, and inspection procedures been written?
- Does new or specialized test equipment need to be purchased?

The quality department is responsible for preparing and distributing a report following each design review. The report form includes these categories:
- Product name and identification number,
- Review number,
- Supplier or provider,

- Review date,
- Attendees' names,
- Product quality attributes discussed,
- Specifications, drawings, bills of materials appended,
- Actions required,
- Assigned to,
- Completion date,
- Prepared by, and
- Approved by.

# ISO 9001 CLAUSE 4.5: DOCUMENT AND DATA CONTROL

## QUALITY RECORDS AND DOCUMENTATION CONTROL

### Purpose

The purpose of this procedure is to describe basic requirements and methods for establishing and maintaining quality records.

### Scope

This procedure applies to all quality documents, including policies, procedures, work instructions, standards, bills of materials, contracts, engineering, standards, and specifications.

### Procedure

Records and documentation are the principal form of objective and reliable quality evidence. The organization's quality records and documentation are maintained in such a manner as to provide operational departments and customers information of the status of the quality initiatives.

The type and amount of quality documentation changes depends on customer and organizational requirements. At a minimum the following record files and documentation are retained:

- *Contracts and customer requirements.* This file is retained in the sales department. Documentation includes all relevant materials necessary to fully understand the customer's needs.

- *Supplier history.* This file is retained in the purchasing department. This documentation includes supplier history, supplier audits, corrective action requests, and cost-quality-service evaluations.

- *Nonconforming material.* This file is retained in the quality department. This file consists of nonconforming shipment reports from suppliers, nonconforming in-process reports, cost-of-quality reports, corrective action requests, and follow-up reports.

- *Process production tooling and equipment.* This file is retained in the manufacturing department. Each piece of equipment and tooling is checked for capability and calibration.

- *Inspection criteria.* This file is retained in the quality control department. Incoming, in-process, and final inspection criteria are in this file. First-article inspection, methods, equipment, sampling instructions, instructions, and special test results are retained in this file.

## ISO 9001 CLAUSE 4.6: PURCHASING

### PURCHASING CONTROLS

#### Purpose

The purpose of this procedure is to establish the requirements for purchasing products, parts, and services.

#### Scope

This procedure applies to all purchased and in-house materials, hardware, software, subassemblies, and assemblies.

#### Procedure

The purchasing and quality departments work together to develop a list of ISO 9000–certified suppliers. ISO 9000–certified suppliers are placed on an approved supplier bidders list. All materials, parts, and services received from noncertified suppliers comply with this procedure.

Purchase documents address the following:
- Drawings,
- Description of product,
- Number of products,
- Quality attributes,
- Inspection instructions,
- Process instructions,
- Packaging and handling instructions,
- Delivery instructions, and
- Other contract requirements.

If quality system requirements and certifications are not specified, the quality and purchasing departments can require product certifications. Product certifications include the following:
- *Parts and products.* Certifications may include testing of product quality attributes, special instructions, and process requirements.
- *Raw material.* Certifications may include mill tests, physical analyses, and chemical analyses.
- *Fabricated parts.* Certifications may include chemical analyses and physical analyses.

All documents relating to supplier quality requirements are included in the bid package sent to suppliers. Purchasing and quality representatives are designated to answer supplier questions.

## SUPPLIER QUALITY EVALUATION

### *Purpose*

This procedure details the requirements for evaluating prospective and existing suppliers to determine their capabilities for producing assemblies, subassemblies, and parts to specified requirements.

## Scope

Any department or business unit may request a supplier quality evaluation. Requests are addressed to either the purchasing or quality department. Supplier evaluations may evaluate quality, technology, cost, delivery, and service capabilities. Suppliers are evaluated prior to and during the contract. External supplier requirements are the same as internal supplier requirements.

## Procedure

Requests for a supplier quality evaluation are addressed to the quality or purchasing department. Either department notifies the other of the request, and both work together to conduct the evaluation. These departments are familiar with the applicable drawings and specifications.

The purchasing department is responsible for making the formal survey arrangements with the supplier. The purchasing department
- Explains the purpose of the evaluation,
- Schedules the audit,
- Identifies the particular areas to be evaluated,
- Discusses special requirements,
- Identifies the particular specifications and requirements to be used, and
- Identifies members of the audit team.

The quality department is responsible for conducting the audit. The quality department works closely with the purchasing department to ensure that it progresses smoothly. The quality department
- Contacts the supplier after purchasing notification,
- Arranges with the supplier to identify a key supplier representative,
- Conducts the audit,
- Briefs the supplier on preliminary findings, and
- Sends the supplier a full report.

The auditor follows the auditing procedure or uses the supplier quality survey form.

## ISO 9001 CLAUSE 4.7: CONTROL OF CUSTOMER-SUPPLIED PRODUCT

### USE OF CUSTOMER PROPERTY

*Purpose*

This procedure details the system for ensuring the integrity of property furnished by the customer.

*Scope*

This procedure applies to customer-furnished material, instruments, and equipment.

*Procedure*

Quality department inspectors examine all customer-furnished materials and instruments by
- Verifying quantities,
- Inspecting for completeness,
- Examining for handling, storage, and transit damage, and
- Examining for proper identification.

Prior to use, testing and measurement equipment is tested to ensure satisfactory operation. Materials and products are functionally tested to ensure satisfactory operation and specification compliance prior to or after installation or assembly.

Quality assurance is responsible for conducting periodic audits to ensure that equipment and materials are properly stored, handled, transported, protected, and maintained. If discrepancies are detected, then quality assurance issues a corrective action request.

Customer property is examined prior to, during, and after usage. Discrepancies are noted. Quality assurance is responsible for notifying the customer about damage, malfunction, miscalibration, misuse, abuse, damage, deterioration. If a discrepancy is detected after assembly or installation, then a corrective action report is issued to indicate probable cause.

## CONTROL OF CUSTOMER PROPERTY

### *Purpose*

The purpose of this procedure is to ensure the efficient and effective control of customer property.

### *Scope*

This procedure applies to all materials, equipment, and property furnished by the customer in order to comply with the contract.

### *Procedure*

Quality control 100 percent inspects all customer-furnished materials, equipment, and property. Quality control also maintains and updates the master list of customer-furnished equipment. The master list details the following information:
- Contract or purchase order identification,
- Equipment description,
- Identification number,
- Quantity received,
- Quantity issued and location, and
- Remaining balance and location.

Quality control is responsible for complying with special customer instructions for the supplied equipment, which may include
- Periodic inspection,
- Periodic maintenance,
- Exposure protection,
- Adjustment,
- Cleaning,
- Proper storage, handling, and preservation, and
- Special tools.

# ISO 9001 CLAUSE 4.8: PRODUCT IDENTIFICATION AND TRACEABILITY

## PRODUCT TRACEABILITY

### *Purpose*

The purpose of this procedure is to detail product identification and traceability.

### *Scope*

This procedure applies to all supplied, production, and other materials.

### *Procedure*

If there is a field problem or a recall, materials and products are positively identified so they can be traced and retrieved. All raw materials used to produce parts, lots, and batches are uniquely identified. Lots and batches of materials are not mixed.

The quality department and the manufacturing department are responsible for ensuring that lots and batches of materials from suppliers are uniquely identified. If materials or parts are tested or stray from the parent batches, then subbatches are uniquely identified. Unique identification may be serial identification through color codes, logs, or tags.

If materials require special testing or processing, then production ensures that testing details are identified on the shipment's or lot's permanent record. Nonstandard treatments of a shipment are also recorded such as rework and repair.

Field repair, installation, modification, or erection processes are also identified on the product tracking sheets.

# ISO 9001 CLAUSE 4.9: PROCESS CONTROL

## PROCESS CONTROL

### *Purpose*

This procedure details the method for monitoring, assessing, and controlling the quality of production processes.

### *Scope*

This procedure applies to internal and to supplier processes.

### *Procedure*

The quality department consults with operating departments to determine which incoming, in-process, and final assessment processes may be controlled.

Prevention is preferred over inspection. Process control is a form of prevention.

Operational departments are responsible for the quality of their operations. The quality department on request provides assistance in solving and correcting operational deficiencies. The quality department also examines documentation and operational plans to determine and to develop criteria for evaluating, monitoring, and controlling processes.

The quality department periodically conducts an internal quality survey of operations. The purpose of the survey is to determine the effectiveness of process control, capability, and improvement.

The results of the internal surveys are sent to the supervisor of the particular operation.

Corrective action and follow-up are the responsibilities of the specific department where the problem occurred. The operational department is responsible for
- Determining causes,
- Correcting symptoms,

- Correcting root causes,
- Monitoring recurrences, and
- Reporting and correcting recurrences.

## FIRST-ARTICLE INSPECTION

### *Purpose*

This procedure defines the requirements for ensuring that the first articles or products from a process or machine satisfy requirements. This ensures the early detection and correction of possible problems.

### *Scope*

This procedure applies to the first articles or products from a production process.

### *Procedure*

First-article inspection is conducted on internal or supplier parts to determine whether the process is capable of meeting specifications.

The supplier sets up a production process to comply with written or engineering design requirements. The requirements may spell out
- Dimensional requirements,
- Functional requirements,
- Performance requirements,
- Physical or chemical characteristics,
- Critical, major, and minor product characteristics,
- Capability requirements, and
- Surface attributes.

Tests are conducted by the supplier, quality assurance, or a third party. Or quality assurance may ensure compliance by observing tests.

Tests, measurements, and inspection are conducted in accordance with approved procedures and instructions. If special tests are required, then the quality department is responsible for selecting, sending, and monitoring the laboratory's performance.

On completion of the tests, the customer is notified of the following:

- Product or part name,
- Product or part number,
- Description of the part,
- Supplier name and purchase order number,
- Name of customer,
- Inspector or tester's name,
- Approval or rejection,
- Results and conclusions,
- Recommended disposition, and
- Attached test results.

Copies of the report are distributed to the
- Customer,
- Supplier,
- Purchasing department, and
- Quality assurance department.

## ISO 9001 CLAUSE 4.10: INSPECTION AND TESTING

### RECEIVING INSPECTION

*Purpose*

This procedure defines the system for inspecting incoming materials from suppliers.

*Scope*

While prevention and process control documentation is the preferred option of controlling supplied-material quality, inspection in restricted cases is still prescribed. The quality assurance department maintains the list of inspected materials.

*Procedure*

All materials and products are inspected for completeness, handling damage, transportation damage, deterioration, documentation, and accurate paperwork. Receiving personnel are responsible for this activity.

In addition, specified materials are inspected for conformance to specified requirements. Requirements are spelled out in specifications, procedures, instructions, purchase orders, engineering drawings, or other documentation. An accurate and complete list of materials is available in the incoming receiving area. Receiving or quality inspection personnel are responsible for this activity.

In addition, specified materials require special tests or analyses. An accurate and complete list of materials to be specially tested is readily available in the incoming receiving area.

Inspectors follow appropriate and the latest inspection instructions, drawings, specifications, and other appropriate reference materials.

Incoming test, measurement, and inspection equipment and devices are forwarded to the quality department for calibration and review.

Materials that have been prequalified or are from certified suppliers are assessed for count, damage, and documentation completeness.

The quality department is responsible for certifying suppliers and developing the approved materials list. Quality personnel periodically audit this list for its completeness and accuracy. The purchasing department is responsible for notifying the supplier of incoming inspection, providing engineering specifications, and providing relevant quality information to suppliers.

Incoming inspectors have the following:
- Engineering drawings,
- Specifications,
- Inspection instructions, and
- Calibrated test and measurement equipment.

On inspection, inspection personnel record results identifying
- Supplier name and purchase order number,
- Invoice number,
- Name and number of product,
- Description of product,
- Quantities,
- Inspector identification,
- Quality criteria (such as critical product attributes),

- Inspection criteria (such as sample size), and
- Inspection results.

Discrepancies are categorized as follows:
- Handling and shipping,
- Product characteristics,
- Paperwork,
- Functional characteristics,
- Fit characteristics, and
- Blemishes.

Materials requiring special testing are noted, such as
- Nondestructive and
- Liquid dye penetrant.

Incoming receiving personnel forward to the appropriate laboratory the specified incoming materials requiring special inspection and testing. The laboratory can be internal or external to the organization. Regardless, the laboratory personnel identify the following:
- Product number and description,
- Quantity,
- Supplier's name,
- Purchase order number,
- Types of tests to be conducted,
- Critical product attributes to be checked,
- Specifications or reference documents,
- Name and location of laboratory,
- Number of products tested,
- Technician's name, and
- Results and conclusions.

Accepted materials are sent to stock or to the production line. Inspector or tester tags or otherwise marks accepted materials. Rejected materials are segregated in the material disposition area. The inspector or tester also tags or otherwise marks rejected materials. Rejected materials may be returned, replaced, or reworked. Inspectors or testers notify the purchasing department and the material review board of the situation. These authorities are responsible for determining the disposition of materials.

* * *

The quality inspector is responsible for updating supplier history records. Rejected shipments automatically trigger a corrective action request and possible audit. The purchasing or quality department determines the need for an audit.

## In-Process Inspection

### Purpose

The purpose of this procedure is to provide guidelines for conducting quality inspections at key points of the process or production line.

### Scope

This procedure applies to manufactured products identified as requiring testing or inspection.

### Procedure

In-process inspection may require
- Evaluation of quality workmanship,
- Determination of conformance to specifications through measurements,
- Examination of physical characteristics,
- Evaluation of certifications,
- Conducting of tests, or
- Evaluation of compliance to special instructions.

Process engineering with the consultation of quality engineering determines and establishes the intervals and points for conducting inspections during the planning phase of the contract. In-process inspections are accomplished at each process step. At in-process location points, critical and major quality product characteristics are also evaluated. If physical or visual inspection is impossible or not required, quality control evaluates process control and process capability. If sufficient control and capability are established, then physical inspection may be waived on approval by quality engineering.

Inspectors are provided with stamps to indicate that the required inspections are conducted.

Instructions are established for each in-process inspection and include acceptance or rejection criteria for each critical and major product quality attribute. Quality control periodically evaluates work instructions and in-process work instructions. Inspectors fill out a nonconforming material report and indicate the status of the material on the manufacturing report.

Quality control reviews all special customer processing instructions to ensure that production is capable of satisfying requirements.

Quality control supervision is responsible for conducting periodic checks and audits of in-process inspections.

## Final Inspection

### *Purpose*

The purpose of this procedure is to provide guidelines for conducting final inspection and testing.

### *Scope*

This procedure applies to specified manufactured products.

### *Procedure*

Quality control is responsible for conducting final inspection and testing and ensuring that all products conform to specifications.

Quality assurance and production personnel jointly develop final inspection and test procedures for products with critical and major characteristics. Final inspection and testing ensure that all customer and contract requirements are satisfied.

If final inspection identifies deficiencies, questionable conditions, flaws, or unusual conditions, then the following parties are immediately notified:
- Design engineering,
- Manufacturing,

- Purchasing, and
- Supplier.

Quality control ensures that the following criteria for final inspection are established:
- Competent inspectors,
- Understandable instructions,
- Calibrated measuring equipment, and
- A clean work area.

Quality control documents the results of all final inspection and testing.

## FINAL TESTING

### *Purpose*

This procedure details the methods, accountability, and authorities for conducting the final acceptance testing of finished products to ensure that they comply with customer requirements.

### *Scope*

This procedure applies to all specified finished products and goods. Quality control is responsible for specifying products that are tested.

### *Procedure*

Quality assurance develops and maintains a current list of all products to be acceptance tested.

Production and manufacturing personnel are responsible for conducting the testing and for determining acceptance or rejection. Quality control is responsible for monitoring calibration.

Production and manufacturing personnel prepare a test report for each product and/or lot of products. The test report identifies
- Part number,
- Lot or batch number,

- Sample size if required,
- Tests conducted,
- Tester's or inspector's name,
- Test specification number,
- Result of the test,
- Recommendation and conclusion, and
- Disposition of the products.

Tested products may be
- Accepted,
- Reworked,
- Scrapped, or
- Returned.

Accepted products are sent to the customer or placed in inventory. Reworked, scrapped, and returned products are identified and segregated. Materials to be reworked are routed to the appropriate department with the test results. Manufacturing personnel notify the quality department for proper disposition of the reworked materials.

# ISO 9001 CLAUSE 4.11: CONTROL OF INSPECTION, MEASURING, AND TEST EQUIPMENT

## CALIBRATION SYSTEM CONTROL

### Purpose

This procedure details the responsibilities and the system for controlling measurement and test equipment.

### Scope

This procedure applies to all departments that use inspection, measurement, and test equipment. The quality department is responsible for operating and maintaining the calibration system.

## *Procedure*

All inspection, test, and measurement equipment and devices that must be calibrated are identified. The list is kept in a master log in the quality department.

The quality department is responsible for identifying measurement equipment to be calibrated, monitoring the calibration system, ensuring proper calibration, maintaining the master calibration log, writing calibration procedures, and specifying the level of precision and accuracy.

Calibration occurs as frequently as required by the customer, regulatory authority, or other parties. The equipment is monitored to ensure that calibration meets these requirements. Calibration frequency is determined by usage, purpose, requirements, process, stability, and environment.

Specified inspection, test, and measurement equipment is calibrated to working measurement standards and then to higher reference measurement standards traceable to the National Institute of Standards and Technology (NIST).

Documentation identifies the following:
- Number and description of the piece of equipment,
- Location of the equipment,
- Measurement specification identification,
- Use of the equipment,
- Date of calibration,
- Identification of the calibrator, and
- Date of the next calibration.

Measurement equipment is uniquely identified and traceable to the above measurement documentation. Calibration identification is color coded, tagged, or given similar marking.

Operating departments are responsible for monitoring calibration status and due dates.

Products tested using uncalibrated or overdue calibrated equipment may be rejected or recalled depending on the use of the products. Operating and quality management are responsible for this determination.

Inspection, test, and measurement equipment that has exceeded calibration due dates cannot be used. It is segregated, and the quality department is notified.

The environment where calibrated equipment is used is also controlled. Environmental controls may apply to temperature, humidity, vibration, and dust.

The purchasing and quality departments are responsible for communicating measurement and calibration requirements and monitoring suppliers' measurement systems.

All specified new, reworked, repaired, and modified measurement equipment is examined, approved, and certified by the quality department.

# ISO 9001 CLAUSE 4:12: INSPECTION AND TEST STATUS

## INSPECTION AND TEST STATUS SYSTEMS

### *Purpose*

The purpose of this procedure is to describe the system for indicating the inspection and test status of materials.

### *Scope*

This procedure applies to all purchased and in-house produced products.

### *Procedure*

Production quality personnel indicate the inspection and test status on purchased and in-house produced products through tags and stamps.

The purpose of the tags or stamps is to indicate the conformance or nonconformance of products following inspection and tests. Quality control is responsible for defining in the quality plan inspection and test status criteria throughout production, installation, and servicing.

Only products with conforming tags and stamps are accepted in the next production step.

❊ ❊ ❊

Inspection and test status stamps and tags are color coded. Green stamps and tags indicate conforming materials. Red stamps and tags indicate nonconforming materials.

Red stamps and/or tags result in a rejection and a disposition report consisting of the following information:
- Part name and number,
- Date of inspection and/or test,
- Person conducting the inspection and/or test,
- Supplier of materials,
- Work order or purchase order number,
- Quantity delivered,
- Inspection criteria and acceptable quality level,
- Quantity inspected,
- Quantity rejected,
- Reason for rejection, and
- Disposition of rejected materials.

# ISO 9001 4.13: CONTROL OF NONCONFORMING PRODUCT

## HANDLING NONCONFORMING MATERIALS

### *Purpose*

This procedure explains the requirements for identifying, controlling, documenting, disposing, and reporting nonconforming materials.

### *Scope*

This procedure applies to all nonconforming materials.

### *Procedure*

All materials not satisfying, conforming to, or complying with requirements are identified and segregated.

❋ ❋ ❋

The quality department representative initiates a nonconforming material report and notifies the responsible parties.

On notification of the nonconforming materials, the quality representative, material review board representative, and responsible party jointly determine whether the materials should be
- Scrapped,
- Returned to the supplier,
- Repaired,
- Reworked, or
- Given a "use as is" waiver.

Scrapped materials are segregated and destroyed per quality department instructions. The following parties are informed of the disposition:
- The material review board,
- Accounting,
- Manufacturing and production,
- Purchasing, and
- The supplier.

Material returned to suppliers requires a corrective action request (CAR). The quality representative initiates the CAR and ensures follow up. The purchasing department informs the supplier about the CAR.

Repaired and reworked materials are sent to production or to inventory on inspection and conformance to specifications of all critical and major characteristics. The following parties are kept informed:
- The material review board,
- Accounting,
- Manufacturing and production,
- Purchasing, and
- The supplier.

"Use as is" waivers are not offered unless
- Deficiencies are minor,
- Operating departments approve, and
- The material review board approves.

## ISO 9001 4.14: CORRECTIVE AND PREVENTIVE ACTION

### Corrective Action Requests

*Purpose*

This procedure details a system for informing personnel about a noncompliance or nonconformance to quality requirements and the need for initiating corrective actions.

*Scope*

This procedure encompasses all activities, departments, internal suppliers, external suppliers, and business units of the organization.

*Procedure*

The quality department is responsible for conducting the audits and for ensuring that the report is transmitted to the appropriate parties.

The auditor is responsible for investigating the cause and recommending the appropriate course of action to eliminate the symptom and the root cause.

A corrective action request (CAR) is initiated as a result of a deficiency or discrepancy. The deficiency may be discovered as a result of an audit or during the normal course of business. The goal of the CAR is to fix the symptom and to eliminate the cause.

The CAR report identifies the following:
- The CAR identification number,
- Name, address, and telephone number of the auditee,
- Name, address, and telephone number of the auditor,
- Name, address, and telephone number of the customer,
- Date of request,
- Date of the audit,
- Project, product, and part number,
- Applicable regulatory or internal specifications,
- A description of the deficiency,
- Symptom and root causes,

- Conclusions, and
- Recommendations.

The quality department maintains the corrective action request (CAR) status log. The log details
- The CAR number,
- Recommendations,
- The name of the organization responsible for correction action,
- Response effectiveness and date, and
- Any recurrence of the problem.

The CAR is transmitted to the customer and auditee. The auditee is responsible for determining the actual cause of the discrepancy and actions taken to prevent recurrence.

The customer or auditee can request a postaudit to determine the effectiveness of the corrective action.

## ISO 9001 CLAUSE 4.15: HANDLING, STORAGE, PACKAGING, PRESERVATION, AND DELIVERY

### PACKAGING, HANDLING, AND SHIPPING RESPONSIBILITIES

*Purpose*

This procedure details responsibilities for controlling the packaging, counting, handling, and shipping of products.

*Scope*

This procedure applies to the packaging, handling, and shipping of all assemblies, products, and spare parts.

*Responsibilities*

The production and purchasing departments are responsible for complying with this procedure.

The production manager is responsible for scheduling and arranging for the movement of products to the stores department. The stores manager is responsible for ensuring the integrity of the packaging, handling, and shipment of products.

Stores personnel are responsible for ensuring the proper count of products in packages.

Drivers are responsible for ensuring that delivered products continue to satisfy specifications and satisfy the customer.

## **HANDLING, STORAGE, PRESERVATION, AND SHIPMENT**

### *Purpose*

The purpose of this procedure is to provide guidelines for the proper and safe handling, storage, preservation, and shipment of materials and products.

### *Scope*

This procedure applies to all materials.

### *Procedure*

The following materials are stored per work instructions:
- Aluminum stock and bar,
- Steel plate,
- Steel tubing, and
- Threaded fittings.

All products are handled, stored, preserved, and shipped according to procedures, work instructions, and the manufacturer's instructions. Shelf-life products are stored and distributed according to first in, first out (FIFO). Identified products are released according to the manufacturer's recommendations. For example, the shelf life of polyethylene plastic is prescribed by the manufacturer's specifications.

Receiving and shipping personnel ensure that care is taken so that products are free from

- Foreign residues,
- Moisture,
- Dirt, and
- Nicks and surface abrasion.

Products with special customer requirements are identified on the special packaging list. Quality control personnel maintain the list and ensure that it is current.

Receiving and shipping personnel notify quality control personnel about product deficiencies. Quality control personnel respond to these notifications and within two working days issue a corrective action request and determine disposition of the materials.

Quality control personnel conduct periodic audits to determine the status and effectiveness of these quality systems.

## ISO 9001 CLAUSE 4.16: CONTROL OF QUALITY RECORDS

### QUALITY RECORDS

#### *Purpose*

The purpose of this procedure is to ensure that quality records are current and accurate.

#### *Scope*

This procedure applies to all company quality records.

#### *Procedure*

The quality department or designated person is responsible for identifying, collecting, indexing, filing, storing, maintaining, and disposing of quality records.

Quality records are maintained to indicate compliance with requirements and quality system effectiveness.

✻ ✻ ✻

The originator and the holder of the quality record is responsible for ensuring that they are accessible, legible, and secured.

The quality department is responsible for establishing and communicating retention times for the quality records.

Quality records are confidential documents and are the exclusive property of the company. They are available for review by customers or suppliers through a formal request to the quality department.

## ISO 9001 CLAUSE 4.17: INTERNAL QUALITY AUDITS

### INTERNAL QUALITY AUDITS

#### *Purpose*

Quality audits are periodically conducted to determine the efficiency and effectiveness of the organization's quality activities.

#### *Scope*

This procedure applies to all internal functions and business units.

#### *Procedure*

The quality department is responsible for conducting the audit. Departmental managers must authorize the audit. The auditee is notified of the pending audit within two weeks.

The audit supervisor or manager reviews and approves the audit plan. A quality audit follows three elements:
- Planning,
- Conducting, and
- Reporting.

The auditor is responsible for developing an audit plan. The audit plan details how the audit is conducted. The plan incorporates the

- Customer or client,
- Auditor's name,
- Auditee's area and name,
- Program or project name,
- ISO 9001 quality system requirement elements,
- Audit date,
- Audit plan or course of action, and
- Reporting procedure.

The quality audit seeks to determine compliance with the appropriate ISO 9001 requirement. The auditor ensures that quality documents satisfy ISO 9000 requirements. First, the quality manual is reviewed for compliance. Business unit or functional area procedures and work instructions are evaluated to determine whether work is performed according to documentation.

The auditor may conduct the following tests:
- Comparing work against work instructions,
- Testing random production products to evaluate the effectiveness of test or production processes,
- Observing work methods to ensure they follow procedures,
- Analyzing deviations or deficiencies to determine cause,
- Calculating stresses, reliability, or other quality-related problems, and
- Inspecting drawings, bills of material, or other technical documentation for accuracy, completeness, and understandability.

If deficiencies are discovered, then they are reported in a corrective action request. Reports are completed within one week of the audit.

Quality audit reports are reviewed by the auditee and approved by quality audit supervision. If required, follow-up audits may be conducted on request.

## CUSTOMER AUDIT AND INSPECTION

### *Purpose*

The purpose of this procedure is to offer guidelines for preparing and responding to customer requests for an audit.

## Scope

This procedure applies to all contracts where the customer is allowed to audit facilities.

## Procedure

Contracts and purchase orders may allow for customer audits, inspections, or other forms of evaluation.

Quality control is responsible for planning and working with the customer audit representative during the audit. Quality control is specifically responsible for
- Understanding customer requirements,
- Notifying internal personnel of these requirements,
- Providing adequate notice to internal personnel of the impending audit, and
- Providing the auditor with space, resources, test results, or any other information.

Customer auditors may request
- An organizational chart,
- A quality manual,
- Quality procedures or work instructions,
- Quality records,
- Corrective actions,
- Drawings and revisions,
- Measuring and testing equipment documentation,
- Control of purchases evidence,
- Materials control evidence,
- Inspection and test results,
- Handling, preservation, storage, and delivery procedures,
- Status analysis,
- Nonconforming material reports,
- Indication of test and inspection status reports, and
- Supplier control evidence.

# ISO 9001 CLAUSE 4.18: TRAINING

## QUALITY TRAINING PROCEDURE

### *Purpose*

This procedure details the requirements for training, certifying, and recertifying new and existing employees in critical and specialized quality functions.

### *Scope*

This procedure applies to personnel who conduct critical specialized tests such as soldering, welding, testing, and inspection. Certification may be required of existing and of new employees. Recertification of the above-specified functions is required annually. If quality systems, methods, machines, controls, and processes change, then recertification may occur more often.

### *Procedure*

The training department is responsible for developing and maintaining training. Operating departments are responsible for ensuring that training adequately covers job requirements. The quality department is responsible for ensuring that training meets ISO 9000 requirements.

New and existing employees are notified of pending sessions one month before training session. Each employee is provided with the
- Purpose of the training,
- Testing requirements,
- Date of the training,
- Subject matter covered in training,
- Location of training, and
- Instructor's name.

If an employee is unable to attend the designated training, then he or she is responsible for rescheduling the training. If the employee has not recertified by the required time, then he or she can't perform the certified function until satisfactory recertification.

Recertification training and sessions cover
- New specifications or requirements,
- New methods of operation or instructions,
- Performance requirements,
- Quality assurance checks, and
- Record keeping.

The instructor must be qualified to conduct the test and to verify satisfactory completion of requirements.

Employees satisfactorily recertified are issued a certification card identifying
- The employee's name,
- The issuance date,
- The expiration date of the certification,
- Tests and functions covered by the certification,
- The certification number, and
- The instructor's name.

Periodically, planned and random performance testing may be conducted. If an employee fails the test, then another test may be conducted. The employee may be reassigned, recertified, retrained, or required to pass the test.

## ISO 9001 CLAUSE 4.19: SERVICING

### AFTER-SALES SERVICING

#### *Purpose*

The purpose of this procedure is to record and control servicing products.

#### *Scope*

This procedure applies to all after-sales servicing of products.

#### *Procedure*

The sales and service department is responsible for servicing products.

❖ ❖ ❖

The quality department is informed of all field failures, breakdowns, or service calls.

All service calls are reported in the service call report, which is transmitted to the quality department.

The purchasing department is informed of the service call in order to obtain spare parts.

All product services follow the procedures detailed in the service manual and product specifications.

The customer, on inspecting and testing the product, signs off on the service.

The quality department initiates a corrective action review of recurring or chronic field failures.

## ISO 9001 CLAUSE 4.20: STATISTICAL TECHNIQUES

### PROCESS CAPABILITY STUDY

#### *Purpose*

The purpose of this procedure is to determine the process capability of new products and processes.

#### *Scope*

Key products from new suppliers.

#### *Procedure*

The engineering manager is responsible for initiating the request of a process capability study on new and modified products and processes. The engineering manager or designated design engineer is responsible for determining the product quality characteristics to be studied.

❊ ❊ ❊

Process capability studies may be initiated for in-house or for supplied products and processes.

The quality manager or designated representative is responsible for ensuring that all critical and major characteristics are fully defined. The quality representative then develops a plan for conducting the process capability study.

The process capability study assesses critical and major process and product characteristics. Capability indices are $Cpk = 1.33$ for critical and major product characteristics. The study entails a minimum production of 60 parts. It is conducted during the manufacture of the preproduction parts.

The process quality engineer studies the process to ensure that the drawings, materials, and other technical data satisfy the customer's specifications.

The process quality engineer ensures that the process is in control. The study is conducted under normal operating conditions. The process engineer, process supervisor, and operator jointly evaluate production equipment, measuring equipment, methods, environment, training, jigs, and other potential sources of variation.

If the process is capable of meeting specifications, production is approved. If the process is not capable, then corrective actions are initiated. Engineering, quality and production personnel jointly evaluate the results of the capability study to determine appropriate actions.

The results of the capability study are recorded in the process capability report.

# SAMPLE QUALITY FORMS

# Acknowledgment of Quality Policies and Procedures

A copy of the policies, procedures, and work instructions manual, number XX, has been sent to you. As the assigned manual holder, you are expected to know and be familiar with the contents of the manual, specifically the following points:

1. The manual holder is responsible for reading, understanding, and implementing the quality procedure and any updates.

2. The manual is the property of the company and must be returned immediately on request.

3. The manual contains proprietary and sensitive information that must not be shared or discussed with anyone outside the company.

4. Any revision or update to the manual is to be read and filed in the manual within two days of receipt of the change.

5. The manual holder is also responsible for communicating the substance of the manual to team members or other work area employees.

_____
Signature

_____
Date

# Approved Supplier List

| CONTRACT/PURCHASE ORDER NUMBER | PREPARATION DATE |
|---|---|
| PURCHASING APPROVED | QUALITY APPROVED |
| DATE APPROVED | DATE APPROVED |

| SUPPLIER NAME AND ADDRESS | PARTS AND SERVICE PROVIDED | PART NUMBER |
|---|---|---|
| | | |
| | | |
| | | |
| | | |
| | | |
| | | |
| | | |

# Calibration Record

| EQUIPMENT IDENTIFICATION NUMBER | EQUIPMENT DESCRIPTION |
|---|---|
| | |

| LOCATION | CALIBRATION INTERVAL |
|---|---|
| | |

| CALIBRATOR NAME | CALIBRATOR ADDRESS |
|---|---|
| | |

| DATE CALIBRATED | AMOUNT OUT OF CALIBRATION | NEXT CALIBRATION DATE |
|---|---|---|
| | | |
| | | |
| | | |
| | | |
| | | |
| | | |
| | | |
| | | |
| | | |
| | | |
| | | |
| | | |

| QA REVIEWED BY | DATE |
|---|---|
| | |
| | |

| **Corrective Action Request (CAR)** ||
|---|---|
| CORRECTIVE ACTION REQUEST NUMBER | AUDIT REQUEST DATE |
| AUDITEE NAME<br><br>LOCATION<br><br>PHONE NUMBER | CUSTOMER NAME<br><br>LOCATION<br><br>PHONE NUMBER |
| PART OR PROCESS NAME | AUDIT NUMBER AND DATE |
| PROCESS DESCRIPTIONS AND LOCATION ||
| DEFICIENCY DESCRIPTION AND LEVELS ||
| DESCRIPTION OF CONDITION ||
| POSSIBLE OR PROBABLE CAUSE ||
| REAL CAUSE ||
| ACTIONS TAKEN TO ELIMINATE CAUSE ||
| AUDITOR SIGNATURE | DATE |
| PERSON RESPONSIBLE FOR CAR | DATE CORRECTED |

## Corrective Action Status Report

| CAR NUMBER | AUDIT NUMBER | AUDITEE NAME | CAR DATE | RECOM-MENDED REPLY DATE | DATE OF REPLY | REMARKS |
|---|---|---|---|---|---|---|
| | | | | | | |
| | | | | | | |
| | | | | | | |
| | | | | | | |
| | | | | | | |
| | | | | | | |

# Customer-Supplied Equipment

| CUSTOMER | | EQUIPMENT DESCRIPTION | |
|---|---|---|---|
| EQUIPMENT IDENTIFICATION NUMBER | | INSPECTOR NAME | |
| DATE RECEIVED | | INSPECTION INTERVAL | |

| INSPECTION DATE | LOCATION | STATUS | DATE IN SERVICE | DATE OUT OF SERVICE |
|---|---|---|---|---|
| | | | | |
| | | | | |
| | | | | |
| | | | | |
| | | | | |
| | | | | |
| | | | | |
| | | | | |

## Employee Quality Training

| EMPLOYEE NAME | | EMPLOYEE IDENTIFICATION NUMBER | |
|---|---|---|---|
| DEPARTMENT/PLANT/BUSINESS UNIT | | DATE | |

| COURSE | COMPLETION DATE | ON-THE-JOB TEST REQUESTED | YEARLY UPDATE |
|---|---|---|---|
| COMPANY POLICIES | | | |
| ISO 9000 | | | |
| CUSTOMER SERVICE | | | |
| SPC (STATISTICAL PROCESS CONTROL) | | | |
| MEASUREMENT AND INSPECTION TOOLS | | | |

# First-Piece Inspection

| PART NAME | PART NUMBER |
|---|---|
|  |  |

| LOT OR SHIPMENT | MACHINE OR PROCESS |
|---|---|
|  |  |

| OPERATOR | DATE |
|---|---|
|  |  |

| PRODUCT CHARACTERISTIC | SPECIFICATIONS OR CAPABILITY | FINDINGS |
|---|---|---|
|  |  |  |
|  |  |  |
|  |  |  |
|  |  |  |
|  |  |  |
|  |  |  |
|  |  |  |
|  |  |  |

CONCLUSIONS AND RECOMMENDATIONS

# Handling, Storage, Packaging, and Delivery Requirements and Instructions

| PART NAME | PART NUMBER |
|---|---|
| CUSTOMER | DRAWING NUMBERS |
| PREPARED BY | DATE |
| SPECIAL HANDLING REQUIREMENTS | ACTIONS REQUIRED |
| SPECIAL STORAGE REQUIREMENTS | ACTIONS REQUIRED |
| SPECIAL PACKAGING REQUIREMENTS | ACTIONS REQUIRED |
| SPECIAL DELIVERY REQUIREMENTS | ACTION REQUIRED |

| **Inspection Instructions** ||
|---|---|
| CUSTOMER | CONTRACT OR PURCHASE ORDER NUMBER |
| PART NUMBER | PART IDENTIFICATION |
| ACCEPTANCE OR REJECTION CRITERIA ||
| INSPECTED BY | APPROVED BY |
| DATE | DATE |

# ISO 9000 Quality Policies

| POLICY OR PROCEDURE TITLE | RESPONSIBLE PERSON | FIRST DRAFT REVIEW DATE | SECOND DRAFT REVIEW DATE | COMPLETION DATE |
|---|---|---|---|---|
| | | | | |
| | | | | |
| | | | | |
| | | | | |
| | | | | |
| | | | | |
| | | | | |
| | | | | |
| | | | | |
| | | | | |
| | | | | |

# ISO 9001 Preassessment Checklist

|  | YES | NO | N/A |
|---|---|---|---|

*1. Management Responsibility*

Is executive management actively involved in quality?
Are quality policies, objectives, and plans developed?
Are quality policies, objectives, and plans understood by employees?
Are quality responsibilities and authorities defined for all personnel?
Do specific employees have responsibility to conduct the following quality activities, including:

   a. Problem identification?
   b. Defect prevention?
   c. Correcting problems?
   d. Ongoing operational control?

Are internal resources allocated and dedicated for quality assessment, design reviews, inspection, and testing?
Are assessment personnel objective and independent of those whose products are assessed?
Has an executive representative been appointed to be responsible for quality and ISO 9000?
Are quality systems processes and products periodically evaluated for effectiveness and continued compliance?
Are sufficient personnel and resources assigned for quality verification activities?
Are sufficient records maintained of organization and management quality activities?

*2. Quality System*

Are quality systems maintained for ensuring that products conform to requirements?
Are all quality systems properly documented?
Does the quality documentation system include policies, procedures, plans, and work instructions?
Is documentation complete, current, and accurate?

*(continued)*

## ISO 9001 Preassessment Checklist (continued)

|  | YES | NO | N/A |
|---|---|---|---|

Are quality policies accumulated in a quality manual?
Are quality plans prepared and used?
Do quality plans address

    a. Identification of quality controls?
    b. Production compatibility?
    c. Updating testing procedures?
    d. Identification of measurement requirements?
    e. Clarification of process and product requirements?
    f. Preparation of quality records?
    g. Identification of verification throughout product development?

*3. Contract Review*

Are contracts prior to acceptance reviewed for capability, compliance, or special requirements?
Are customer requirements fully defined?
Are customer requirements fully understood?
Are differences between customer and supplier resolved?
Are contract modifications reviewed?
Are contract and customer requirements records maintained?

*4. Design Control*

Are procedures developed to control and verify product design?
Does the design satisfy customer requirements?
Are plans developed to identify accountabilities and authorities for development of the design?
Are design plans checked and updated throughout the product-development cycle?
Is the design periodically checked and otherwise verified by qualified personnel?
Are technical, organizational, and other interfaces identified?

*(continued)*

## ISO 9001 Preassessment Checklist (continued)

|  | YES | NO | N/A |
|---|---|---|---|
| Are design input, output, and verification requirements identified and resolved? | | | |
| Are design conflicts resolved effectively? | | | |
| Does design output satisfy input requirements? | | | |
| Are there reference or benchmark criteria for design input and output? | | | |
| Are reference and benchmark criteria satisfied? | | | |
| Are designs checked for regulatory or governmental compliance? | | | |
| Are criteria and major product characteristics identified? | | | |
| Are designs verified by competent and independent personnel? | | | |
| Are calculations checked? | | | |
| Are qualification tests conducted? | | | |
| Are design changes verified and approved? | | | |
| Is there sufficient documentation for controlling design and design modifications? | | | |
| **5. Document and Data Control** | | | |
| Are paper and electronic design and quality-related documents and critical data controlled? | | | |
| Are documents and data reviewed and approved by authorized personnel? | | | |
| Are quality documents and data available to appropriate parties? | | | |
| Are obsolete documents and data removed from use? | | | |
| Is there a master list of approved documents? | | | |
| Is the master list accurate and up to date? | | | |
| Is there an approved distribution list for documents and critical data? | | | |
| Are changes to documents and data reviewed and approved by the same personnel initiating the documents? | | | |
| Are changes to designs and documents properly reviewed? | | | |
| Are changes identified on engineering drawings? | | | |
| Is there a master list for controlling documents and critical data? | | | |

*(continued)*

| **ISO 9001 Preassessment Checklist** (continued) | YES | NO | N/A |
|---|---|---|---|
| Are documents and data reissued after changes have been made? | | | |
| 6. *Purchasing* | | | |
| Are purchased products assessed and monitored for compliance to requirements? | | | |
| Are suppliers evaluated and monitored over the life of the project? | | | |
| Are supplier records current, complete, and accurate? | | | |
| Are quality system controls for purchased materials effective and efficient? | | | |
| Are customer purchasing documents complete and understandable? | | | |
| Are products fully described and identified? | | | |
| Are purchasing documents periodically reviewed and approved by authorized personnel? | | | |
| Can the customer verify the quality of purchased products through on-site audits? | | | |
| Do suppliers understand customer requirements? | | | |
| Do suppliers' suppliers fully understand customer requirements? | | | |
| 7. *Control of Customer-Supplied Product* | | | |
| Does the supplier provide documentation of the verification, storage, and maintenance of customer-supplied products? | | | |
| Is there sufficient documentation (a paper trail) identifying the quality of customer-supplied products? | | | |
| 8. *Product Identification and Traceability* | | | |
| Are products identified and traceable throughout the production, delivery, and installation processes? | | | |
| Are products traceable by specific batches or lots? | | | |
| 9. *Process Control* | | | |
| Are critical production, installation, and servicing quality processes in control and capable? | | | |

(*continued*)

## ISO 9001 Preassessment Checklist (continued)

|  | YES | NO | N/A |
|---|---|---|---|
| Are the concepts of control, capability, and improvement understood? | | | |
| Are critical and major quality areas clearly identified? | | | |
| Do procedures define key quality processes? | | | |
| Are quality standards and reference documents identified? | | | |
| Are key product quality characteristics identified? | | | |
| Are key process variables relating to these quality product characteristics controlled? | | | |
| Are processes and equipment approved by authorized personnel? | | | |
| Are process and equipment changes approved by authorized personnel? | | | |
| Are process and equipment changes approved by authorized personnel? | | | |
| Are there workmanship instructions? | | | |
| Are personnel certified? | | | |
| Are all critical process quality requirements specified? | | | |
| Does documentation exist for suitably controlling processes? | | | |
| *10. Inspection and Testing* | | | |
| Are incoming products tested and inspected? | | | |
| Are there other forms of certification? | | | |
| Does inspection or verification follow a quality plan? | | | |
| Are inspection and testing results properly identified and documented? | | | |
| Are receiving inspection and testing evaluated for effectiveness? | | | |
| Are incoming inspection requirements related to the supplier's capability? | | | |
| If a recall is required, can all products be retrieved? | | | |
| Are in-process testing and inspection conducted? | | | |
| Do in-process testing and inspection follow a plan? | | | |
| Are major quality processes controlled and monitored? | | | |
| Are major quality processes in control, capable, and improving? | | | |
| Are products segregated until testing has been completed? | | | |
| Are nonconforming materials properly identified? | | | |

*(continued)*

| **ISO 9001 Preassessment Checklist** (continued) | | | |
|---|---|---|---|
| | YES | NO | N/A |
| Do final inspection and testing follow a quality plan? | | | |
| Are products tested for conformance to customer requirements? | | | |
| Are accurate and current records maintained on test and inspection status and results? | | | |
| *11. Control of Inspection, Measuring, and Test Equipment* | | | |
| Is inspection, measurement, and test equipment controlled and calibrated? | | | |
| Is the testing and measurement equipment capable of performing required measurements? | | | |
| Are the reliability and repeatability of the measurement equipment known? | | | |
| Are the types of measurements specified? | | | |
| Are the accuracy and precision of the instruments specified? | | | |
| Is test and measurement equipment calibrated at prescribed intervals? | | | |
| Is calibrated test and measurement equipment traceable to national standards? | | | |
| If there are no national or international standards, is the rationale for calibration defined? | | | |
| Do procedures specify the location, identification, acceptance criteria, frequency of verification, and type of verification of test and measurement equipment? | | | |
| Is calibration status positively identified? | | | |
| Are calibration records maintained current, and accurate for inspection, measurement, and test equipment? | | | |
| Are inspection and measurements periodically assessed for accuracy? | | | |
| Are environmental conditions suitable for accurate testing and measurement? | | | |
| Are handling and storage methods for test and measurement equipment specified? | | | |
| Are test hardware and software calibrated? | | | |
| Are test hardware and software capable of accurate and precise measurements? | | | |

*(continued)*

| **ISO 9001 Preassessment Checklist** (*continued*) | YES | NO | N/A |
|---|---|---|---|
| Do the quality plan or documentation procedures indicate inspection and test status? | | | |
| Is identification maintained throughout production and installation of the product? | | | |
| Does documentation record responsibility and authority for releasing products? | | | |
| *13. Control of Nonconforming Product* | | | |
| Are procedures established for ensuring that nonconforming products are not used or installed? | | | |
| Have nonconforming products been released and used? | | | |
| Are nonconforming products identified, documented, evaluated, segregated, and disposed of properly? | | | |
| Are all parties informed about nonconforming products? | | | |
| Are authority and responsibility for determining and disposing of nonconforming products defined? | | | |
| Are nonconforming products reviewed according to procedures? | | | |
| Are rework, acceptance, rejection, and regrade of products specified? | | | |
| Are nonconforming products ever used? | | | |
| Are procedures developed and followed for the use of nonconforming products? | | | |
| Are reworked or repaired products reinspected according to procedures? | | | |
| *14. Corrective and Preventive Action* | | | |
| Are corrective and preventive action procedures developed and consistently followed? | | | |
| Are preventive actions planned companywide? | | | |
| Are the symptoms and causes of nonconforming products eliminated? | | | |
| Are customer complaints followed up? | | | |
| Are processes and reports investigated for determining patterns of failure? | | | |
| Are internal controls implemented after corrective action to ensure that problems don't recur? | | | |

(*continued*)

## ISO 9001 Preassessment Checklist *(continued)*

|  | YES | NO | N/A |
|---|---|---|---|
| Are postaudits conducted to determine the effectiveness of corrective action? | | | |
| Are procedures rewritten to reflect changes taken due to corrective and preventive action? | | | |
| *15. Handling, Storage, Packaging, Preservation, and Delivery* | | | |
| Do procedures specify proper handling, storage, packaging, and delivery? | | | |
| Are there adequate means for handling materials? | | | |
| Are products stored safely? | | | |
| Are there adequate procedures for preventing damage or deterioration of products? | | | |
| Are the conditions of products in inventory periodically evaluated? | | | |
| Is the preservation of products documented? | | | |
| Does packaging protect products? | | | |
| *16. Control of Quality Records* | | | |
| Are there documented procedures for identifying, collecting, and storing quality records? | | | |
| Are quality documents and records accurate and current? | | | |
| Are suppliers' records and suppliers' suppliers' records accurate and current? | | | |
| Are quality records accessible? | | | |
| Are quality records retained for sufficient time? | | | |
| Are quality records available to the customer and other interested parties? | | | |
| *17. Internal Quality Audits* | | | |
| Are internal quality audits conducted? | | | |
| Are internal quality audits properly planned, conducted, and reported? | | | |
| Are audits prioritized? | | | |
| Is there corrective action as a result of the audits? | | | |
| Is corrective action effectiveness monitored? | | | |
| Does top management review the effectiveness of corrective action? | | | |

*(continued)*

| **ISO 9001 Preassessment Checklist** (continued) | | | |
|---|---|---|---|
| | YES | NO | N/A |
| 18. *Training* <br> Are training needs identified and documented? <br> Are training resources adequate for the internal training needs? <br> Are all personnel trained in quality technologies? <br> Are training records maintained? | | | |
| 19. *Servicing* <br> Are there service requirements in the contract? <br> Are customer complaints recorded and handled? <br> Are contractual service requirements complied with? <br> Are there procedures for satisfying and verifying contractual requirements? | | | |
| 20. *Statistical Techniques* <br> Are statistical techniques used in the organization? <br> Are statistical techniques used for determining production control, capability, and improvement? <br> Is statistical process control used? | | | |

# ISO 9001 Quality Evaluation Checklist

| PART NAME | PART NUMBER |
|---|---|
| CUSTOMER OR PURCHASE ORDER NUMBER | DRAWING NUMBER |
| PURCHASED BY | DATE |

| ITEM | REQUIRED | AVAILABLE |
|---|---|---|
| ENGINEERING PRINTS | | |
| BILLS OF MATERIALS | | |
| AS-BUILT DRAWINGS | | |
| ASSEMBLY DIRECTIONS | | |
| OPERATING INSTRUCTIONS | | |
| MAINTENANCE INSTRUCTIONS | | |
| FINAL TEST DATA | | |
| PHYSICAL TESTS | | |
| CHEMICAL TESTS | | |
| CERTIFICATIONS | | |
| PRODUCT TESTS | | |
| QUALITY AUDITS | | |
| CAR RESULTS | | |

# Machined Parts Instruction Form

| PART NAME | | | PART NUMBER | | |
|---|---|---|---|---|---|
| CUSTOMER OR DOWNSTREAM PROCESS | | | SUPPLIER OR UPSTREAM PROCESS | | |
| INSPECTION DATE | | | APPROVED BY | | |
| PRODUCT CHARAC- TERISTIC | LOT SIZE | SAMPLE SIZE | NUMBER REJECTED | ACCEPT/ REJECT | REMARKS |
| | | | | | |
| | | | | | |
| | | | | | |
| | | | | | |
| | | | | | |
| | | | | | |
| | | | | | |
| | | | | | |

| **New Product Analysis** ||
|---|---|
| CUSTOMER | CONTRACT OR PURCHASE ORDER NUMBER |
| PRODUCT DESCRIPTION | PRODUCTION START DATE |
| PRODUCTION QUANTITY | MONTHLY DELIVERY RATE |
| SIMILARITY TO PREVIOUS CONTRACT (EXPLAIN IF YES) ||
| ARE QUALITY REQUIREMENTS SPELLED OUT? ||
| SUMMARIZE CONTRACT QUALITY REQUIREMENTS ||
| SPECIAL INSPECTION, MEASUREMENT, OR TEST EQUIPMENT ||
| SPECIAL INSTRUCTIONS OR METHODS ||
| SPECIAL SKILLS OR CERTIFICATIONS ||
| OPERATOR OR INSPECTOR REQUIREMENTS ||
| SPECIAL ENVIRONMENTAL REQUIREMENTS ||
| OTHER REQUIREMENTS ||
| PREPARED BY ||

## Nonconforming Materials and Parts Report

| | |
|---|---|
| CONTRACT OR PURCHASE ORDER NUMBER | DATE |
| DRAWING NUMBER | PREPARED BY |
| PART NUMBER | PART NAME |
| WORK ORDER NUMBER | DEPARTMENT OR SUPPLIER RESPONSIBLE |
| LOT NUMBER | NUMBER OF PRODUCTS IN LOT |
| NUMBER INSPECTED | NUMBER REJECTED |
| DEFICIENCY FINDINGS | |
| DISPOSITION (SCRAP/REWORK/REPAIR/RETURN TO SUPPLIER) | |
| CORRECTIVE ACTION REQUIREMENTS | |
| APPROVED BY | DATE |

## Nonconforming Materials Master Log

| LOG DATE | DISPOSITION DATE | PART NUMBER | PART NAME | ACTIONS TAKEN |
|---|---|---|---|---|
| | | | | |
| | | | | |
| | | | | |
| | | | | |
| | | | | |
| | | | | |
| | | | | |
| | | | | |

| **Organizational Commitment Statement** |
|---|
| MANUAL HOLDER<br><br>TITLE<br><br>DATE<br><br>ORGANIZATION<br><br>CONTROLLED DOCUMENT<br><br>This quality procedures manual is the property of Alpha, Incorporated. This manual is assigned to the above position. On termination or transfer of your employment, the manual is to be returned to Alpha, Inc. Revisions to the quality manual are read, understood, implemented, and filed into this manual. Revisions to the quality policies manual are not permitted without the quality vice president's authorization. |

# Process and Production Instructions

| CUSTOMER | CONTRACT OR PURCHASE ORDER NUMBER | APPROVED BY | DATE |
|---|---|---|---|
| | | | |

| PART NUMBER | PART NAME | LOT NUMBER | QUANTITY | WORK ORDER NUMBER |
|---|---|---|---|---|
| | | | | |

| ENGINEERING DRAWING OR REVISION NUMBER | MATERIALS REQUESTED | ASSEMBLY DRAWING NUMBER |
|---|---|---|
| | | |

| SEQUENCE NUMBER | TOOLING | WORK DESIGN | EMPLOYEE NUMBER | QUALITY OR INSPECTOR | STANDBY HOURS | ACTUAL HOURS |
|---|---|---|---|---|---|---|
| | | | | | | |
| | | | | | | |
| | | | | | | |
| | | | | | | |
| | | | | | | |
| | | | | | | |

## Process, Production, Inspection, and Measurement Equipment Maintenance

| EQUIPMENT IDENTIFICATION NUMBER | MAINTENANCE REQUIRED | COST OF MAINTENANCE | DATE COMPLETED | COMPLETED BY |
|---|---|---|---|---|
| | | | | |
| | | | | |
| | | | | |
| | | | | |
| | | | | |
| | | | | |
| | | | | |
| | | | | |
| | | | | |
| | | | | |
| | | | | |

# Quality Assurance Plan

| CUSTOMER | | CONTRACT OR PURCHASE ORDER NUMBER | |
|---|---|---|---|
| PART NUMBER | | PART IDENTIFICATION NUMBER | |
| QUALITY ACTIVITIES | INSPECTION OR TEST EQUIPMENT | RESPONSIBLE PARTY | TIME REQUIREMENTS |
|  |  |  |  |
| PREPARED BY | | APPROVED BY | |
| DATE | | DATE | |

## Quality Manual Approval List

President _____

Vice President Quality _____

Vice President Manufacturing _____

Vice President Purchasing _____

Vice President Finance _____

Plant Manager 1 _____

Plant Manager 2 _____

The vice president of quality is the designated management representative with the authority and responsibility of developing, approving, implementing, and revising the quality procedures in this quality procedures manual.

## Quality Manual Table of Contents

| SECTION NUMBER | TITLE | ISO 9001 REFERENCE NUMBER | REVISION |
|---|---|---|---|
| Section 0 | Organizational Commitment | 4.0 | B |
| Section 1 | Management Responsibility | 4.1 | B |
| Section 2 | Quality System | 4.2 | B |
| Section 3 | Contract Review | 4.3 | B |
| Section 4 | Design Control | 4.4 | B |
| Section 5 | Document and Data Control | 4.5 | B |
| Section 6 | Purchasing | 4.6 | B |
| Section 7 | Control of Customer-Supplied Product | 4.7 | B |
| Section 8 | Product Identification and Traceability | 4.8 | B |
| Section 9 | Process Control | 4.9 | B |
| Section 10 | Inspection and Testing | 4.10 | B |
| Section 11 | Control of Inspection, Measuring, and Test Equipment | 4.11 | B |
| Section 12 | Inspection and Test Status | 4.12 | B |
| Section 13 | Control of Nonconforming Product | 4.13 | B |
| Section 14 | Corrective and Preventive Action | 4.14 | B |
| Section 15 | Handling, Storage, Packaging, Preservation, and Delivery | 4.15 | B |
| Section 16 | Control of Quality Records | 4.16 | B |
| Section 17 | Internal Quality Audits | 4.17 | B |
| Section 18 | Training | 4.18 | B |
| Section 19 | Servicing | 4.19 | B |
| Section 20 | Statistical Techniques | 4.20 | B |

| Quality Policies Approval and Review Chart | | | |
|---|---|---|---|
| ISO 9000 POLICY REQUEST | 1ST REVIEW AND APPROVAL | 2ND REVIEW AND APPROVAL | 3RD REVIEW AND APPROVAL |
| MANAGEMENT RESPONSIBILITY | | | |
| QUALITY SYSTEM | | | |
| CONTRACT REVIEW | | | |
| DESIGN CONTROL | | | |
| DOCUMENT AND DATA CONTROL | | | |
| PURCHASING | | | |
| CONTROL OF CUSTOMER-SUPPLIED PRODUCT | | | |
| PRODUCT IDENTIFICATION AND TRACEABILITY | | | |
| PROCESS CONTROL | | | |
| INSPECTION AND TESTING | | | |

*(continued)*

| Quality Policies Approval and Review Chart *(continued)* ||||
|---|---|---|---|
| ISO 9000 POLICY REQUEST | 1ST REVIEW AND APPROVAL | 2ND REVIEW AND APPROVAL | 3RD REVIEW AND APPROVAL |
| CONTROL OF INSPECTION, MEASURING, AND TEST EQUIPMENT | | | |
| INSPECTION AND TEST STATUS | | | |
| CONTROL OF NONCONFORMING PRODUCT | | | |
| CORRECTIVE AND PREVENTIVE ACTION | | | |
| HANDLING, STORAGE, PACKAGING, PRESERVATION, AND DELIVERY | | | |
| CONTROL OF QUALITY RECORDS | | | |
| INTERNAL QUALITY AUDITS | | | |
| TRAINING | | | |
| SERVICING | | | |
| STATISTICAL TECHNIQUES | | | |

# Receiving, In-Process, and Final Inspection Instructions

| PART NAME | PART NUMBER |
|---|---|
| | |

| CUSTOMER OR DOWNSTREAM PROCESS | SUPPLIER OR UPSTREAM PROCESS |
|---|---|
| | |

| DATE | APPROVED BY |
|---|---|
| | |

| PRODUCT CRITICAL OR MAJOR CHARACTERISTIC | ACCEPTABLE QUALITY LEVEL | TEST METHODS | DRAWINGS/SPECS/ STANDARDS |
|---|---|---|---|
| | | | |
| | | | |
| | | | |
| | | | |
| | | | |
| | | | |
| | | | |

| **Waiver or Deviation Request** ||
|---|---|
| REQUEST NUMBER | DATE |
| CUSTOMER OR PURCHASE ORDER NUMBER | REQUESTER |

| PART NAME | PART NUMBER | SPECIFICATIONS OR DRAWINGS |
|---|---|---|
|  |  |  |

Reason for Deviation or Waiver (identify specific product attributes)

| REQUESTED BY | DATE |
|---|---|
| APPROVED BY (customer) | DATE |

# GLOSSARY

ISO 9000 has its own language. The International Organization for Standardization (ISO) is a worldwide federation of more than ninety national standards development bodies. This global reach allows the development of common terms and concepts, which is critically important in the development of quality.

As the maintenance, control, and improvement of quality become trade issues, more people are using quality terms that sometimes differ in meaning depending on who is using the term and in what context. Different companies use terms that are specific to their industry. Quality pundits, gurus, consultants, and other interested parties also use terms a little differently, sometimes resulting in misunderstanding and confusion.

ISO has done a remarkable job in standardizing quality terms and concepts. The definitions in this book follow those detailed in ISO 8402.

What is quality? Although *quality* is a basic term, it still causes confusion and much debate. The following are commonly included in definitions of quality:

- Conformance or compliance with requirement,
- Degree of excellence,
- Highest value, and
- Customer satisfaction.

Confusion also surrounds such terms as *total quality management, quality assurance*, and *quality control*. Unless the basic terms are defined, confusion results.

Many quality terms and concepts are used in this book and usually are understandable in context. In this glossary, these quality terms and concepts are thoroughly defined.

**Auditee.**  Area, person, or process being evaluated or audited.

**Auditor.**  Person qualified to conduct quality assessments or audits. Also called *quality assessor*.

**CAR.**  Acronym for *corrective action request*. Recommendation by the auditor for an auditee to correct a deficiency in an ISO 9000 quality system requirement.

**Calibration.**  Comparison, correlation, and adjustment between two test instruments where one of the test instruments has known accuracy.

**Calibration control.**  Documented system for ensuring that inspection, test, and measurement equipment is calibrated according to procedures and has the required accuracy and precision and that deviations from requirements are corrected.

**Calibration interval.**  Interval between calibrations.

**Certification.**  Qualification or approval for new or existing inspection, test, and measurement equipment to ensure that its accuracy and precision comply with requirements.

**Conformance assessment.**  Testing or evaluating the service, product, or process to establish compliance with requirements. Also called *conformity assessment*.

**Conformity.**  Ability to satisfy specified requirements.

**Contract review.**  Systematic analysis by a supplier of a customer's quality requirement and the ability to satisfy the contract.

**Corrective action.**  Activities taken to eliminate the causes of a nonconformance or recurrence of a nonconformance.

**Customer.**  Recipient of a product or service provided by a supplier. In older ISO 9001/9002/9003 standards, the customer was also called the *purchaser*.

**Defect.** Inability to satisfy requirements, usually surrounding the issue of safety. Often, *defect, deficiency*, and *nonconformity* are used synonymously.

**Design review.** Complete and detailed assessment of a design to ensure that it can meet customer requirements for quality and other factors. The review identifies existing and possible problems and supplies solutions to them.

**Grade.** Rank given to a product or service to indicate relative differences. Grades can range from very high to commodity.

**Harmonization.** Term used for standardization in order to create national, regional, and international product compatibility and transparency.

**Hold point.** Area or station at which materials, equipment, or documents can't proceed until actions have been taken. Actions may be testing, verification, measurement, or authorization.

**Inspection.** Ensuring compliance or conformance to requirements. Inspection involves examining, testing, measurement, and other assessment activities.

**Interchangeability.** Ability to be used by other functions or entities with the same result.

**ISO 9000.** Formal standard title is "Quality Management and Quality Assurance Standards: Guidelines for Selection and Use."

**ISO 9001.** Formal standard title is "Quality Systems Model for Quality Assurance in Design/Development, Production, Installation, and Servicing,"

**ISO 9002.** Formal standard title is "Quality Systems: Model for Quality Assurance in Products and Installation."

**ISO 9003.** Formal standard title is "Quality Systems Model for Quality Assurance in Final Inspection and Test."

**ISO 9004.** Formal standard title is "Quality Management and Quality System Elements—Guidelines."

**ISO 9000 registrars.** Bodies recognized, approved, or certified to conduct ISO 900 quality system audits and to maintain lists of approved suppliers.

**Management review.** Formal assessment by senior management of the efficiency and effectiveness of the quality system

**Material review board (MRB).** An internal board consisting of operating departments that reviews materials, evaluates suppliers, authorizes audits, and determines disposition of nonconforming materials.

**Measurement reference.** Measurement, inspection, and test equipment that is tested against a higher or primary standard of reference, such as those traceable to the National Institute of Standards and Technology.

**Measurement transfer.** Measurement, inspection, and test equipment that is used to test and to transfer measurements from a higher accurate and precise piece of equipment to a less accurate and precise piece of equipment.

**Measuring and test equipment.** Equipment used to measure, gauge, test, inspect, or examine products for conformance with specifications.

**Nonconforming material.** Any product, part, or assembly that has one or more quality characteristics that do not conform to a specification, drawing, or other requirement.

**Procedure.** Preferred, approved, or specified manner in which an activity or action is performed.

**Process.** Interrelated operations changing inputs into outputs. Operations involve using resources—including people, methods, and equipment—efficiently.

**Quality.** In the ISO 9000 universe, quality is the ability to comply or conform to requirements. Also, quality is the ability to satisfy customer requirements.

**Quality assurance.** Planned operational and organizational activities ensuring that quality activities are planned and customer requirements are satisfied.

**Quality audit.** Planned, objective, independent, and systematic examination of quality and operational activities. Audits may evaluate compliance, control, maintenance, efficiency, or effectiveness.

**Quality audit stages.** Three stages of the quality audit are planning, implementation, and reporting or closure.

**Quality control.** Operational and process regulation of activities surrounding quality. Control implies maintenance, monitoring, and improvement of processes, systems, and products.

**Quality costs.** Quality costing structure consisting of prevention, correction, internal failure, and external failure costs.

**Quality improvement.** Actions taken primarily to enhance organizational, process, and product quality. This also includes enhancing the organization's efficiency, effectiveness, and economy.

**Quality management.** Companywide quality activities including quality assurance, quality control, inspection, planning, and other senior-level activities.

**Quality planning.** Internal activities that ensure that customer requirements are identified and satisfied.

**Quality policies.** Companywide directives regarding quality. Quality policies are included in the quality manual.

**Quality requirements.** Specifications, usually of the customer, relating to quality. These are often itemized in a contract or purchase order.

**Quality system.** ISO 9000 quality systems include documentation, processes, resources, methods, equipment, environment, and other quality-related activities that are used to satisfy requirements.

**Quality system documentation.** Documents describing organizational quality efforts. May include a quality manual, procedures, work instructions, engineering prints, and quality standards.

**Registration.** Procedure by which a recognized body verifies that applicable process, service, or product characteristics conform to ISO 9000 requirements. The recognized body maintains lists and ensures capability of its auditors. Also called *quality systems certification*.

**Record.** Documented facts relating to a specific activity, person, or place.

**Repair.** Action or activity that fixes a product nonconformance so that it fulfills user fitness requirements.

**Rework.** Action or activity that fixes a product nonconformance so that it meets original requirements.

**Sampling plan.** A statistics-based plan indicating the number of products from a shipment to be selected and inspected and the criteria for acceptance.

**Scrap.**  Nonconforming material that is not usable and cannot be cost-effectively reworked or repaired.

**Self-inspection.**  Ensuring conformance by the person conducting the work.

**Specification.**  Document stating customer requirements. Specifications may include drawings, bills of materials, standards, and other quality-related documents.

**Statistical process control (SPC).**  Statistical method for monitoring, correcting, and improving processes.

**Subcontractor.**  Provider of a product or service to the supplier. Also called the subsupplier or first-tier supplier of the immediate customer.

**Supplier.**  Provider of a product or service to a customer. In older ISO 9001/9002/9003 standards, the supplier was also called the *contractor*.

**Total quality management.**  Management philosophy and methodology centered around the use of quality to satisfy the needs of an organization's stakeholders. Stakeholders may include customers, regulatory authorities, suppliers, community, employees, and management.

**Traceability.**  Ability to track or to identify. Usually, traceability refers to equipment, documents, material, calibration, or other required verification.

**Use-as-is material.**  Material with a minor nonconformance that is waived or approved for use.

**Validation.**  Acquisition of evidence that requirements are being satisfied. Often, validation occurs in final inspection.

**Verification.**  Acquisition of evidence that requirements are being satisfied.

**Waiver.**  Authorization to deviate from a procedure or other type of instruction. Also called a *deviation permit*.

# INDEX

## A

Acknowledgment of Quality Policies and Procedures form, sample of, 143
Administration, of quality policies and procedures, 18–19
After-sales servicing, sample procedure for, 138–39
Americans with Disabilities Act, quality documentation complying with, 15–16
Appendix, in quality manual, 9
Approved Supplier List form, sample of, 144
Audits, *see* Internal quality audits

## B

Binding, of quality manual, 9

## C

Calibration Record form, sample of, 145
Calibration system control, sample procedure for, 125–27
CAR, *see* Corrective Action Request form
Changes
  communicating, 16

Changes (*cont.*)
  in quality documentation, 18, 20
  to quality manual, 13–14
Communicating
  changes, 16
  policies, 14–15
Communications vehicle, quality manual as, 4
Compliance audits, 15
Computers, for quality documentation, 20
Contract review (ISO 9001: 4.3)
  in Preassessment Checklist, 155
  sample procedure for, 104–5
  in sample quality manuals, 34, 50–51, 73, 92
Coordination team, quality policies developed and written by, 13
Corrective Action Request (CAR) form
  sample of, 146
  in sample quality manuals, 63, 85, 95
Corrective Action Status Report form, sample of, 147
Corrective and preventive action (ISO 9001: 4.14)
  in Preassessment Checklist, 160–61
  sample procedure for, 130–31
  in sample quality manuals, 42–43, 63, 84–85, 95
Culture device, quality manual as, 4–5
Customer audit and inspection, sample procedure for, 135–36

Customer property, control of, sample procedure for, 115
Customer property, use of, sample procedure for, 114–15
Customer quality requirements, quality manual and, 8
Customer-Supplied Equipment form, sample of, 148
Customer-supplied product, control of (ISO 9001: 4.7)
   in Preassessment Checklist, 157
   sample procedure for, 114–15
   in sample quality manuals, 38, 56, 76, 93

## D

Data control, *see* Document and data control
Decimal system, quality manual organized by, 7
Definitions, in quality manual, 9
Delivery (ISO 9001: 4.15)
   in Preassessment Checklist, 161
   sample procedure for, 131–33
   in sample quality manuals, 43, 64, 85–86, 95
Delivery Requirements form, sample of, 151
Design control (ISO 9001: 4.4)
   in Preassessment Checklist, 155–56
   sample procedure for, 106–10
   in sample quality manuals, 35–36, 51–53, 93
Design review, sample procedure for, 107–10
Desk audit, of quality manual, 6, 21
Development, of quality manual, 12–13
Document and data control (ISO 9001: 4.5)
   in Preassessment Checklist, 156–57
   sample procedure for, 110–11

Document and data control (*cont.*)
   in sample quality manuals, 36, 53–54, 74–75, 93

## E

Employee Quality Training form, sample of, 149
Engineering drawing review, sample procedure for, 106–7
   *see also* Quality engineering
Equal opportunity regulations, quality documentation complying with, 15–16

## F

Final inspection, sample procedure for, 123–24
Final testing, sample procedure for, 124–25
First-article inspection, sample procedure for, 118–19
First-Piece Inspection form, sample of, 150
Forms, *see* Quality forms

## G

Guidelines for Developing Quality Manuals (ISO 10013), 10

## H

Handling (ISO 9001: 4.15)
   in Preassessment Checklist, 161
   sample procedure for, 131–33
   in sample quality manuals, 43, 64, 85–86, 95

Handling Requirements form, sample of, 151
History of company, in quality manual, 8
Human resource department, quality documentation training by, 15

# I

Identification, *see* Product identification
Implementation, changes in, 16
In-process inspection, sample procedure for, 122–23
Inspection, definition of, 3
Inspection and test status (ISO 9001: 4.12)
   sample procedure for, 127–28
   in sample quality manuals, 41, 61, 82–83, 95
Inspection and testing (ISO 9001: 4.10)
   in Preassessment Checklist, 158–59
   sample procedure for, 118–25
   in sample quality manuals, 39–40, 58–59, 79–80, 94
Inspection equipment, control of (ISO 9001: 4.11)
   in Preassessment Checklist, 159–60
   sample procedure for, 125–27
   in sample quality manuals, 40–41, 59–61, 80–82, 95
Inspection Instructions form, sample of, 152
Instructions, *see* Work instructions
Internal quality audits
   of quality documentation, 11
   quality manual as roadmap for, 6
Internal quality audits (ISO 9001:4.17)
   in Preassessment Checklist, 161
   sample procedure for, 134–36
   in sample quality manuals, 44–45, 65–66, 87–88, 96
ISO 8402, quality terms in, 22

ISO 9000 committee, quality manual developed by and revised by, 10–11, 12–13
ISO 9000 Quality Policies form, sample of, 153
ISO 9000 technical committee, quality terms developed by, 22
ISO 9001
   procedures and, 26
   Quality manual requirements in, 25, 26
ISO 9001 Preassessment Checklist form, sample of, 154–62
ISO 9001 Quality Evaluation Checklist form, sample of, 163
ISO 9001/9002/9003
   quality documentation corresponding to numbering of, 6
   quality manual following, 21–22
   quality system documentation requirements in, 26
   quality system requirements of, 21
   shall requirements in, 19, 21
ISO 9001: 4.1 (management responsibility)
   in Preassessment Checklist, 154
   sample procedure for, 99–100
   in sample quality manuals, 31–32, 47–49, 69–71, 91–92
ISO 9001: 4.2 (quality system)
   in Preassessment Checklist, 154–55
   sample procedure for, 101–3
   in sample quality manuals, 32–34, 49–50, 70–71, 92
ISO 9001: 4.3 (contract review)
   in Preassessment Checklist, 155
   sample procedure for, 104–5
   in sample quality manuals, 34, 50–51, 73, 92
ISO 9001: 4.4 (design control)
   in Preassessment Checklist, 155–56
   sample procedure for, 106–10
   in sample quality manuals, 35–36, 51–53, 93

ISO 9001: 4.5 (document and data control)
   in Preassessment Checklist, 156–57
   sample procedure for, 110–11
   in sample quality manuals, 36, 53–54, 74–75, 93

ISO 9001: 4.6 (purchasing)
   in Preassessment Checklist, 157
   sample procedure for, 111–13
   in sample quality manuals, 37–38, 55–56, 75, 93

ISO 9001: 4.7 (control of customer-supplied product)
   in Preassessment Checklist, 157
   sample procedure for, 114–15
   in sample quality manuals, 38, 56, 76, 93

ISO 9001: 4.8 (product identification and traceability)
   in Preassessment Checklist, 157
   sample procedure for, 116
   in sample quality manuals, 38, 56–57, 77, 93–94

ISO 9001: 4.9 (process control)
   in Preassessment Checklist, 157–58
   sample procedure for, 117–19
   in sample quality manuals, 38–39, 57–58, 78–79, 94

ISO 9001: 4.10 (inspection and testing)
   in Preassessment Checklist, 158–59
   sample procedure for, 118–25
   in sample quality manuals, 39–40, 58–59, 79–80, 94

ISO 9001: 4.11 (control of inspection, measuring, and test equipment)
   in Preassessment Checklist, 159–60
   sample procedure for, 125–27
   in sample quality manuals, 40–41, 59–61, 80–82, 95

ISO 9001: 4.12 (inspection and test status)
   sample procedure for, 127–28

ISO 9001: 4.12 (*cont.*)
   in sample quality manuals, 41, 61, 82–83, 95

ISO 9001: 4.13 (control of nonconforming product)
   in Preassessment Checklist, 160
   sample procedure for, 128–29
   in sample quality manuals, 41–42, 62, 83–84, 95

ISO 9001: 9.14 (corrective and preventive action)
   in Preassessment Checklist, 160–61
   sample procedure for, 130–31
   in sample quality manuals, 42–43, 63, 84–85, 95

ISO 9001: 4.15 (handling, storage, packaging, preservation, and delivery)
   in Preassessment Checklist, 161
   sample procedure for, 131–33
   in sample quality manuals, 43, 64, 85–86, 95

ISO 9001: 4.16 (control of quality records)
   in Preassessment Checklist, 161
   sample procedure for, 133–34
   in sample quality manuals, 44, 64–65, 86–87, 96

ISO 9001: 4.17 (internal quality audits)
   in Preassessment Checklist, 161
   sample procedure for, 134–36
   in sample quality manuals, 44–45, 65–66, 87–88, 96

ISO 9001: 4.18 (training)
   in Preassessment Checklist, 162
   sample procedure for, 137–38
   in sample quality manuals, 45, 66–67, 88–89, 96

ISO 9001: 4.19 (servicing)
   in Preassessment Checklist, 162
   sample procedure for, 138–39
   in sample quality manuals, 46, 67, 96

ISO 9001: 4.20 (statistical techniques)
in Preassessment Checklist, 162
sample procedure for, 139–40
in sample quality manuals, 46, 68, 89–90, 96
ISO 10013 (Guidelines for Developing Quality Manuals), 10

## K

Key concepts, in quality manual, 9
KISS (Keep It Short and Simple) principle, for quality manual development, 23

## L

Lawyers, quality documentation reviewed by, 15–16
Lower-level documentation, audit of, 11

## M

Machined Parts Instruction form, sample of, 164
Management, quality documentation training by, 15
*see also* Quality management; Senior management
Management responsibility (ISO 9001: 4.1)
in Preassessment Checklist, 154
sample procedure for, 99–100
in sample quality manuals, 31–32, 47–49, 69–71, 91–92
Marketing tool, quality manuals as, 9, 21
Measuring equipment, control of (ISO 9001: 4.11)
in Preassessment Checklist, 159–60

Measuring equipment, control of (*cont.*)
sample procedure for, 125–27
in sample quality manuals, 40–41, 59–61, 80–82, 95

## N

Neutral language, in quality manual, 22
New Product Analysis form, sample of, 165
Nonconforming Materials and Parts Report form, sample of, 166
Nonconforming Materials Master Log form, sample of, 167
Nonconforming product, control of (ISO 9001: 4.13)
in Preassessment Checklist, 160
sample procedure for, 128–29
in sample quality manuals, 41–42, 62, 83–84, 95
Numbering, of quality manual, 6–7

## O

Organization chart, in quality manual, 8
Organizational Commitment Statement form, sample of, 168

## P

Packaging (ISO 9001: 4.15)
in Preassessment Checklist, 161
sample procedure for, 131–33
in sample quality manuals, 43, 64, 85–86, 95
Packaging Requirements form, sample of, 151
Page numbering, of quality manual, 9
Paper-based quality system, 20

PAR, *see* Preventive Action Request form
People, importance of working with, 17
*see also* Teams
Peripheral documents, in appendix of quality manual, 9
Policies, *see* Quality policies
Policy committee, quality policy and procedures administered by, 18–19
Preassessment Checklist form, sample of, 154–62
Preservation (ISO 9001: 4.15)
   in Preassessment Checklist, 161
   sample procedure for, 131–33
   in sample quality manuals, 43, 64, 85–86, 95
Preventive action, *see* Corrective and preventive action
Preventive Action Request (PAR) form
   sample procedure for, 130–31
   in sample quality manuals, 63
Procedures, *see* Quality procedures
Process, Production, Inspection, and Measurement Equipment Maintenance form, sample of, 170
Process and Production Instructions form, sample of, 169
Process capability study, sample procedure for, 139–40
Process control (ISO 9001: 4.9)
   in Preassessment Checklist, 157–58
   sample procedure for, 117–19
   in sample quality manuals, 38–39, 57–58, 78–79, 94
Product identification and traceability (ISO 9001: 4.8)
   in Preassessment Checklist, 157
   sample procedure for, 116
   in sample quality manuals, 38, 56–57, 77, 93–94
Purchasing controls, sample procedure for, 111–12
Purchasing (ISO 9001: 4.6)
   in Preassessment Checklist, 157

Purchasing (*cont.*)
   sample procedure for, 111–13
   in sample quality manuals, 37–38, 55–56, 75, 93

## Q

Quality assurance, sample procedure for, 100
Quality Assurance Plan form, sample of, 171
Quality audits, *see* Internal quality audits
Quality classes, quality concepts introduced in, 15
Quality control, sample procedure for, 100
Quality department organization, sample procedure for, 99–100
Quality documentation, 12
   challenges of, 24
   changes in, 16, 18, 20
   computerization of, 20
   consequences of lack of, 23
   distribution of, 19
   ISO 9001/9002/9003 and, 26
   legal review of, 15–16
   organization of, 6–7
   in sample quality manuals, 33, 50, 72
   in team environment, 17, 19
   training for use of, 15
   updating, 15, 19
   *see also* Quality records, control of
Quality documentation audit, 11
Quality engineering, sample procedure for, 99–100
Quality forms, 25, 63, 85, 95, 130–31
   purpose of, 23
   in quality documentation hierarchy, 22
   in sample quality manuals, 33, 50
   samples of, 27, 141–77

# INDEX

Quality management, sample procedure for, 99
  *see also under* Management
Quality Manual Approval List form, sample of, 172
Quality manual assessment, 6, 21
Quality Manual Table of Contents form, sample of, 173
Quality manuals
  as accurate, 22
  as appealing, 21
  appendix in, 8
  approval of, 13–14
  average life of, 11
  binding of, 9
  buy-in into, 22
  changes incorporated into, 14
  common quality terms used in, 22
  as comprehensive, 20, 22
  definition, 3
  definitions in, 8
  description of organization in, 8
  desk audit (assessment) of, 6, 21
  development of, 12–13
  distribution of, 14
  as grammatically correct, 21
  Guidelines for Developing Quality Manuals developed for, 10
  history of company in, 8
  ISO 9001 and, 25, 26
  iterative development process for, 21
  key concepts in, 8
  KISS principle for, 21, 22
  lower-level, 10
  as marketing tool, 9, 21
  master copy for, 21
  neutral language in, 22
  numbering, 6–7
  page numbering for, 9
  in quality documentation hierarchy, 22
  revising, 10–11
  samples of, 25–26, 31–96
  scope in, 8
  site quality, 10

Quality manuals (*cont.*)
  structure of, 7–10
  table of contents, 9, 173
  as tailored to company, 12, 21–22, 24
  template for, 21
  tips for developing, 20–23
  as understandable, 20, 22
  updating, 15, 19
  as usable, 21
  uses of, 4–6
Quality organization personnel, in sample quality manual, 31, 47–48, 70, 92
Quality planning
  sample procedure for, 101–2
  in sample quality manuals, 33
Quality policies
  administration of, 18–19
  communicating, 14–15
  definition, 3–4
  development of, 12–13, 14
  function of, 18
  as generic, 11–12
  numbering, 6–7
  purpose of, 22
  standard operating practices becoming, 14
Quality Policies Approval and Review Chart form, sample of, 174
Quality procedural manuals, 10
Quality procedures
  administration of, 18–19
  audit of, 11
  benefits of, 27
  communicating, 14–15
  definition, 3
  developing, 14
  function of, 18
  integrated into existing procedures, 20
  need for consistent implementation of, 15
  numbering, 6–7
  purpose of, 23

Quality procedures (*cont.*)
  in quality documentation hierarchy, 22
  quality procedural manuals for, 10
  for quality systems requirements, 12
  requirements for, 26–27
  sample of, 26–27, 97–140
  in sample quality manuals, 33, 50, 72, 92
  as specific, 11, 12
  teams and, 17
Quality records, control of (ISO 9001: 4.16)
  in Preassessment Checklist, 161
  sample procedure for, 110–11, 133–34
  in sample quality manuals, 33, 44, 50, 64–65, 86–87, 96
Quality system (ISO 9001: 4.2)
  in Preassessment Checklist, 154–55
  sample procedure for, 101–3
  in sample quality manuals, 32–34, 49–50, 70–71, 92
Quality systems planning, sample procedure for, 102–3
Quality systems requirements, procedures for each, 12
Quality terms, in ISO 8402, 22
Quality vice president or representative, policy committee established by, 18

## R

Receiving, In-process, and Final Inspection Instructions form, sample of, 176
Receiving inspection, sample procedure for, 119–22
Records, *see* Quality records, control of
Registration, communicating need for, 19–20
Regulations, quality documentation complying with, 15–16
Revision, of quality manual, 10–11

## S

Scope, of quality manual, 8
Security clearances, quality documentation needing, 15
Senior management, quality manual development and, 13
  *see also under* Management
Servicing (ISO 9001: 4.19)
  in Preassessment Checklist, 162
  sample procedure for, 138–39
  in sample quality manuals, 46, 67, 96
Shall requirements, ISO 9001/9002/9003 having, 19
Shipping, sample procedure for, 131–33
Standard operating practices, as policies, 14
Statistical techniques (ISO 9001: 4.20)
  in Preassessment Checklist, 162
  sample procedure for, 139–40
  in sample quality manuals, 46, 68, 89–90, 96
Storage (ISO 9001: 4.15)
  in Preassessment Checklist, 161
  sample procedure for, 131–33
  in sample quality manuals, 43, 64, 85–86, 95
Storage Requirements form, sample of, 151
Supplier quality evaluation, sample procedure for, 112–13
Suppliers, in sample quality manuals, 37–38, 55–56, 75, 93
  *see also under* Purchasing

## T

Table of contents, in quality manual, 9, 173
Teams, quality documentation integrated into, 17, 19
Test equipment, control of (ISO 9001: 4.11)

Test equipment, control of (*cont.*)
   in Preassessment Checklist, 159–60
   sample procedure for, 125–27
   in sample quality manuals, 40–41, 59–61, 80–82, 95
Test status, *see* Inspection and test status
Testing, *see* Inspection and testing
Traceability, *see* Product identification and traceability
Training, for quality documentation use, 15
Training (ISO 9001: 4.18)
   in Preassessment Checklist, 162
   sample procedure for, 137–38
   in sample quality manuals, 45, 66–67, 88–89, 96
Training manual, quality manual as, 4

## W

Waiver or Deviation Request form, sample of, 177
Work instructions, 25
   audit of, 11
   communicating, 14–15
   definition, 3, 12
   integrated into existing procedures, 20
   need for consistent implementation of, 15
   numbering, 6–7
   purpose of, 23
   in quality documentation hierarchy, 22
   in sample quality manuals, 33, 50, 72, 92

Made in the USA
Lexington, KY
08 February 2017